I'm Just A Man...

And Other Excuses For Avoiding God

Dr. Casondra. R'. Robinson

The Destiny Road Warrior Companion Book

2018

Copyright © 2018 by Dr. Casondra R'. Robinson

All rights reserved. This book or any portion thereof may not be reproduced or used in any manner whatsoever without the express written permission of the publisher except for the use of brief quotations in a book review or scholarly journal.

First Printing: 2018
ISBN: 0692901841
ISBN – 13: 978-0692701847
Destiny Road Warrior, Inc.
P.O. Box 2431
Conway, AR 72033
www.DestinyRoadWarrior.com

DEDICATION

I dedicate this book to YOU. It takes bravery to consider the possibility that there is something within you that needs change and have the wisdom to seek a source.

Therefore, I am honored and thank you for choosing to allow me the opportunity to pour into the wondrous marvel that is your DESTINY. My dear reader please understand what I already know; that your DESTINY is happening right now.

How far you travel the DESTINY ROAD is your personal freewill decision; but know that God has already put everything you need within you.

Let Him take you all the way

To the point of hearing Him say

"Well done, good and faithful servant" (Matthew 25:23)

For every your accomplishment along the way.

Just A Man In Christ,
Dr. Casondra R'. Robinson

ACKNOWLEDGEMENTS

Everyone needs encouragers & I thank for God the threads that wove beautiful patterns into the fabric that is my life.

My Beloved Children: Bright Eyes, Punki Pi, Mookie, his lovely Jen & the baby of my babies, my Beautiful Butterfly.

My Five Delicious Slices Of Perfection Pi: Nessa Jo, Lijah Bob, Mackie Beau, Sophie Lou Mae & Sammy Lou Junyah aka Zeke.

My Parents, Roger L. Robinson II & Rosalyn Pruitt Armstrong.

My Maternal Grandparents Samuel and Mavis Posey: Some of my happiest & safest memories where under your roof.

My Great-Grandmother Lula James McKeever: You taught me who I was to God, that laughter was the source of my strength, gave me a love for His work & desire for His wisdom. You taught me how to survive the "Thems" and "Those" who would follow.

My Paternal Aunts and Uncles Larry & Mary Wilbert and Charles & Evelyn Cummings: You remembered and loved me, even when I was made to feel invisible by relatives who pretended I did not exist.

My Spiritual Mom, The late Mrs. Della Newborn: You were that which I had been so long without and I am grateful to God for the blessing of you.

My Cover In The Spirit Realm, Pastor Josephus & 1st Lady Shirley King: Covered – upheld – counseled with – consoled – encouraged – prayed for – advised and loved – I am all of these things with you.

My Spirit Realm Mentor & Mom, Chief Apostle Pollyette Parker-Elliot. The Spirit of our Lord rest deep within you Mother Apostle, making my heart & soul continuously rejoice at the blessing of you.

My Spiritual Leaders under whose direction I flourish, Bishop M. L. & Dr. Kimberly Clay. You are excellent gardeners who have created the perfect soil for my soul to grow, multiply and expand.

My Childhood Pastors J. C. Crenshaw, John H. Corbitt & Curtis Ridout: I am still influenced by your teachings and act of kindness.

My Childhood Sunday School Teacher Mrs. Rozenia Jones: You continued to be my teacher long after my own children were taller than you.

My Red Circle Leader Mrs. Belinda Jeffries Ford: An earthbound guardian angel for a misused and abused child.

Minister Of Music, Mrs. Edith Yancy Powell: My childhood choir director who taught the meaning of the song, before the music. She is truly a Shero who greatly inspired my methodology in ministry.

A PRAYER OF GRATITUDE

Dearest Heavenly Father, I enter into Your presence abounding with joy beyond description, humbly submitting my life to Your instruction and care.

Thank You for Your love for me. I am yet alive and well, though the enemy foretold the opposite, multiple times throughout my life.

Thank you for reaching down into the dark place I was held captive, rescuing me and becoming my ark of safety from the storm.

Thank you for giving me beauty for my ashes, being the source of joy that has steeled my spine, sharpened my sword and strengthened my heart to live, fight and leave this life carrying Your banner.

Thank you for teaching me to fallaciousness of unforgiveness, if I want the right to absolution and for taking every moment of my life and turning it into the moment of me being the person I am in you.

I pray for the readers of this book. Let them find a good word within it's pages draws them closer to You. Meet the desire of every heart that longs to dive deeper into relationship with You.

Help each reader to find the Destiny Road which You constructed just for them. Guide them along to the olive tree of faith, where they can sit in the shade of Your love, protected from the scorching heat of this system of things.

In the name of Jesus Christ, who because of Your love for us, took off His crown of glory, put on a crown of thorns, traded it for a crown of victory, that we may return to You. Amen, Amen, Amen.

TABLE OF CONTENTS

I'm Just A Man……….…………………………………………..…1
Reflect, Process & Journal…………………………………...9
I'm Just A Nobody……………………………………………..20
    Ruth: Just Another Nobody………..…………..…………...21
    Reflect, Process & Journal………..…………..…….………..26
    Gideon: Just Another Nobody………..…………..………...31
    Reflect, Process & Journal………..……………..…………..37
I'm Trying To Find Myself.……………..……………….…..43
    Reflect, Process & Journal………..…………..……………...47
Liar, Liar, Pants On Fire!..53
    Reflect, Process & Journal………..…………..……………..62
I Have A "Dis"–Ability………………………………………..69
    Reflect, Process & Journal………..…………..……………..73
        Mental Disability: The Clinically Diagnosed………74
        Mental Disability: The Mentally Challenged……..75
        Emotional Disability………………………………...79
        Physical Disability………..……..…………..……...83
My Past Won't Let Me Have A Future………………………..84
    Reflect, Process & Journal………..…………..……………..87
        The Truth About Pookie, Re Re & The Gang……...89
        A Few More Responses………..……..…………….90
I'm A Person Of Ill Repute……………………………………..92
    Rehab's Confession………..…..……………………………..93
    Ballam's Confession……………..……..……………………..95
    Reflect, Process & Journal………..…………..……………..102
I Have A Criminal Record……………………..……..……..105
    Jake's Story…………………………………………………..106
    King David's Story Of Sex, Lies & Murder………..……...113
    Saint Peter Had A Violent & Potential Deadly Temper…..114
    Moses: A Killer Who Lived Life On The Lam For 40 Yrs.115
    Before Saul Became Paul…………………..……..………...115
    Saul The Serial Killer………………………………….……..116
    Paul The Convict………………….   ………..…....117
    Reflect, Process & Journal………..…………..……………..119

I Was Abused As A Child And Can't Move Past It...................123
    Reflect, Process & Journal......................................154
    A Prayer Of Forgiveness & Release...........................158
I Know I'm Called, I Just Ain't Answering The Phone..............160
    Age...161
    Education..162
    Credibility...162
    Outward Perceptions...163
    Family Support..163
    Reflect, Process & Journal..165
And Finally...168
    What To Do When The Lord Speaks.........................169
    A Prophet's Blessing...170
Resources For Inner Freedom......................................171- 4
About The Author

I'm Just A Man

I'm Just A Man

There was this wealthy fellow who had everything going for him. He, his wife & their three sons were all happily married. His three boys were well educated and had joined him in the family business. They weren't just bringing home the bacon; they were bringing home the whole hog. As a result, their wives were blissfully comfortable and trusted completely in their husbands.

Sounds pretty good, huh? But then it happens…suddenly, the old man starts hearing somebody talking to him; which would have been fine, except nobody in the room had said nary a mumbling word.

Now not only does he listen to his "invisible friend"; but…hold on to your hats folks…he begins to have entire conversations with him. As a matter fact, it was so convincing, that his family believed in his invisible friend, "Mr. IF" for short.

Whatever Mr. IF told him to do, he did it; and did it in public too! After one particular conversation with the air, our friend shut down the family business, liquidated his assets and took his boys to the middle of a large dry pasture far from any body of water. "Well boy's" he said "Mr. IF said to build a cruise ship right here".

Dr. Casondra R'. Robinson

Needless to say, his neighbors were outraged. Here was a fellow pillar of their community acting as if his elevator didn't go to the top floor. Property values plummeted and they couldn't even get out of their driveways because of the media frenzy and all the looky-loos.

To make matters even worse, the old coot was giving interviews to anybody that would listen. He claimed this Mr. IF fellow was a powerful friend to anybody who showed themselves friendly and would stick closer to you than a brother.

This great and powerful Mr. IF was going to do something that had never been done before; make water fall from the sky. Now anybody well traveled had seen a waterfall, but even the village idiot knew that water does not just fall from the sky. Yet there he stood, inviting everybody far and near to pack up and book a room on the lido deck.

Today we call grown folks with invisible friends schizophrenic. If they're in our family, we try to keep it a secret and talk about it in hushed voices. We make sure their socks match, never leave them alone with the baby, explain their behavior as "special" and speak to them using words with eight letters or less when explaining why they should not marry and reproduce.

I'm Just A Man

However, if it's someone from Deacon Udon'tsay's family, it's very different. You couldn't get "Jesus on the main line" if you tried, because you're too busy on the party line getting, giving & adding to the details. Being the good person you are, you don't forget to throw in phrases like "Lord bless his heart", "We all have our cross to bear" & "Don't you leave your kids with that fool!"

Now back to our fellow…Needless to say his "Chicken Little" complex was the butt of many jokes and not one person bought neither swimwear, nor sun block. They were much too sane to take a cruise to crazy town with their neighbor who was apparently the new mayor.

Wait a minute…what the heck is THAT SMELL?!! It smells like a big ol' funky pile of…where did all these animals come from? Oh great! Now the cruise ship has become the world's first zoo! "Close the window Marge and call the sheriff! I know he's on his property, but there's got to be something in the zoning laws about this. What the heck are we paying taxes for?!"

Well the next thing you know, that crazy man and his whole crazy family packed their crazy luggage and boarded that crazy land-locked ocean liner full of crazy animals. Well…at least once the door slammed shut, the air smelled respectable again. It smelled so good, that some said it was a new kind of air.

Even though it caused achy joints in some, it was most refreshing."Marge! Call the contractor, our sprinkling system is going haywire! What do you mean it's not on? Where else could all this water be coming fr…Uhh…Hey there you crazy ol' coot...I mean Mr. Noah, Sir...(blub, blub, blub)…I was just joking! (blub, blub, blub, blub) I believed in your Mr. IF all along… (Blub, Blub, blub, blub, Blub) I was just testing you to see if YOU believed in him (BLUB…. BLUB…BLUB…)

Jumping ahead; the whole world took a big ol' blub, blub, bubble bath. The only ones left breathing was that small group of crazy people, on that crazy boat, full of those crazy (not to mention funky) animals. So, it turns out that Mr. IF was real. He was a real friend, who although not visible to the eyes, was audible to anyone willing to listen.

After docking the boat on the side of a mountain, Mr. IF told the old man to hold the first backyard barbecue and the party was on. Now sometimes, when we've come out on the other side of life's occasional storms, we tend to party a little too much. I won't go into

I'm Just A Man

too much detail, because that would be impolite, but let's just say the old man got a little too deep in his cups and started a one person nudist colony. Trust me when I say it was not a pretty sight and just thank me for not giving you the details.……you're welcome.

I live in a place many people have migrated to. Some came by Mayflower, some came by slave ship; some came through Ellis Island, some came through airport customs. Some even came on inner tubes and rickety rafts. We are all different in many ways, however, we all have one thing in common; we are all descendants of the naked mayor of crazy town who had the faith to build a cruise ship & portable zoo in the middle of a dry, dusty field.

There's no shame in being nuts, as long as you are screwed onto the right bolt. That being said…HOWDY COUSIN!!!

All that begetting they did back then, is how mankind be done begot to us now.

Dr. Casondra R'. Robinson

"This is the book of the generations of Adam…
And Adam lived a hundred and thirty years
And begat a son in his own likeness,
After his image; and called his name Seth:
Seth begat Enos
Enos begat Cainan
Cainan begat Mahalaleel
Mahalaleel begat Jared
Jared begat Enoch
Enoch begat Methuselah
Methuselah begat Lamech
Lamech begat Noah"

Genesis 5:1-29

"These are the generations of Noah. Noah was JUST A MAN…
Noah walked with God."

Genesis 6:9

I'm Just A Man

*"So God created **MAN** in His own image, in the image of God created He him; **MALE AND FEMALE** created He them."*

Genesis 1:27

I threw in that last verse to clear up any confusion about the difference between huMANity and gender. When you saw the picture on the cover of this book, it probably looked contradictory to the title. It was only when you looked beyond my cover that you could see my humanity beyond my gender, which in turn speaks to your humanity.

I am just a man…one man; and yet you are reading my book. You are just one man, be you male or female. Are you living your destiny? If not, what's your excuse?

REFLECT PROCESS & JOURNAL

I'm Just A Man

Write about a situation in your life where everything seemed perfect & then something strange, unexpected and potentially embarrassing happened that turned it all upside down. _____

_____
_____
_____
_____
_____
_____

What was your first reaction? _____
_____
_____
_____
_____

……

If you shared with others, what was their response? _____
_____
_____
_____

Did you try to keep it from public knowledge and if so, why? ___
_____
_____

Imagine how Noah's family felt when this first occurred. But they began to believe in Mr. IF too, so something must have happened to strike a cord within them.

Give an example of a thought you had and you knew wasn't **YOUR** regular way of thinking:_____
_____
_____
_____

*"For behold, He who forms mountains, And creates the wind, Who declares to man what **his** thought is, and makes the morning darkness, Who treads the high places of the earth ~ The LORD God of hosts is His name."* (Lower case "he", "his" & "him" refers to man, not God)

Amos 4:13

I'm Just A Man

Write about a time when you <u>just knew</u> something...without explanation, or what was about to happen, meaning before it happened. Some call this intuition: _____

_____

_____

_____

_____

"Then the LORD answered Job out of the whirlwind, and said: Who is this who darkens counsel By words without knowledge? Now prepare yourself like a man; I will question you, and you shall answer Me. Who has put wisdom in the mind? OR who has given understanding to the heart?"

Job 38:1-3 & 36

"For God gives wisdom and knowledge and joy to a man who is good in His sight..."

Ecclesiastes 2:26

Dr. Casondra R'. Robinson

Now write about a time you went to sleep with a question in your heart and woke up with the answer: _____

_____
_____
_____
_____

"But while he thought about these things, behold, an angel of the LORD appeared to him in a dream, saying, "Joseph, son of David, do not be afraid to take to you Mary your wife, for that which is conceived in her is of the Holy Spirit. And she will bring forth a Son and you shall call His name JESUS, for He will save His people from their sins." So all this was done that it might be fulfilled which was spoken by the Lord through the prophet, saying; "Behold, the virgin shall be with child, and bear a Son, and they shall call His name Immanuel," which is translated, "God with us."

Matthew 1:20-23

I'm Just A Man

Let's hear about one of the dreams you had that later came true:

_____
_____
_____
_____
_____

"And it shall come to pass afterward that I will pour out My Spirit on ***all*** *flesh;...Your old men shall dream dreams..."* (Speaks to humanity wrapped within gender)

Joel 2:28-29

"And it shall come to pass in the last days, says God, that I will pour out of My Spirit on ***all*** *flesh;...Your old men shall dream dreams.*

Acts 2:17

Jot down anytime you've ever had a flash of something not actually happening at the time, that later came to pass: _____
_____

Dr. Casondra R'. Robinson

_____

_____

"And it shall come to pass afterward that I will pour out My Spirit on all flesh; Your sons and your daughters shall prophesy..."

Joel 2:28

"And it shall come to pass in the last days, says God, That I will pour out of My Spirit on all flesh; Your sons and your daughters shall prophesy...and on My menservants and on My maidservants I will pour out My Spirit in those days; and they shall prophesy."

Acts 2:17

"...for prophecy never came by the will of man, but holy men of God spoke as they were moved by the Holy Spirit."

2 Peter 1:21

Write about an incident when you had a conversation with someone, who without realizing it, spoke wisdom concerning an

I'm Just A Man

issue that had been privately weighing on your mind: _____
_____
_____
_____

"The mouth of the righteous speaks wisdom, and his tongue talks of justice"

Psalms 37:30

"Walk in wisdom toward those who are outside, redeeming the time. Let your speech always be with grace, seasoned with salt, that you may know how you ought to answer each one."

Colossians 4:5-6

Write about an instance when your were in an iffy or troubling circumstance, and then for reasons you didn't understand, you were just filled with a sense of peace: _____
_____
_____

"And let the peace of God rule in your hearts, to which also you were called in one body; and be thankful."

Colossians 3:15

These are just some of the ways that the Holy Spirit of the Lord speaks to us. This therefore, is another reason to study your bible – to weigh whether or not what came to you, lines up with the word & will of God.

Every time it does, try to get familiar with the feeling that occurs on a soul level, at the time it occurs. This will likewise familiarize you with the voice and presence of God, opening you to more readily receiving His instruction.

The more you recognize the sender is God, the quicker you can follow Noah's example and obey. Just understand that sometimes it means you have to ignore peer pressure & the way of the world around you. Your obedience will provide you, and your house a haven of safety when the storms of life arise. There are only two options in the time of these storms:

A.   Ride the waves in an ark of safety that only God can imagine for you

B   Sink alongside those who tripped over that which God imagined for you

A Warning:

   If what you received does not line up with the word & will of God, get familiar with the feeling that occurs on a soul level at the time of receipt. This will likewise familiarize you with the voice and presence of satan, and thus train you to immediately rebuke him, along with his taunts, doubts, harassment & wrong instruction.

   Remember everything in the spirit realm is opposite of the mortal realm; meaning you **WANT** to be on the waves with Jesus during the storms of life, and satan banished to be in the place where God is not aka dry shore of the dark place, where the light of living water does not exist.

Dr. Casondra R'. Robinson

"...Then Peter got down out of the boat, walked on the water and came toward Jesus. But when he saw the wind, he was afraid and, beginning to sink, cried out, "Lord, save me!" Immediately Jesus reached out His hand and caught him. "You of litte faith," He said, "why did you doubt?" And when they climbed into the boat, the wind dies down..."

Matthew 14:29-32

"When an unclean spirit is gone out of a man, it goes through dry places,
seeking rest, and findeth none."

Matthew 12:43

"Don't become partners with those who reject God. How can you make a partnership out of right and wrong? That's not partnership; that's war. Is light best friends with dark? Does Christ go strolling with the Devil? Do trust and mistrust hold hands? Who would think of setting up pagan idols in God's holy Temple? But that is exactly what we are, each of us a temple in who God lives."

2 Corinthians 6:14-17 (MSG)

I'm Just A Man

Take a deep breath ~ blow it out and write your thoughts about anything your learned, noticed or related to yourself: _____

_____
_____
_____
_____
_____
_____
_____
_____
_____
_____
_____
_____
_____
_____

I'M JUST A NOBODY

RUTH

God does not prepare only those with position; but He does position all those whom He prepares. Naomi was a widow with no living husband or sons to care for her. Of her two daughter-in-laws, one returned to her parent's house to retry her luck in the dating pool. The only person remaining was Ruth, a grown woman with a Hebrew baby name which meant "friendly and cute".

If you were suddenly on your own in the cruel, tough world, who would you want to accompany you?

A. "Friendly" & "Cute"
B. "Six-Gun" & "Razor Blade"

Before you pick Six-Gun & Razor Blade, I must tell you that Ruth was loyal to Naomi. That's why although she had no husband or sons to protect her, she chose to support her mother-in-law by becoming like many today, a lowly migrant farm worker, an alien in a foreign land.

She could have easily returned with her sister-in-law Orpah to their homeland & found another husband to care for her. But she was faithful to both Naomi and her marriage covenant. Therefore she was determined to care for her, as she would her own mother.

Dr. Casondra Robinson

"Ask me not to leave you, not to turn back from following you: for wherever you go, I shall go; wherever you live, I shall live: your people shall be my people and your God shall be my God. In whatever land you die, there shall I die and be buried. The Lord do so to me and more also if anything other than death separate me from you."

Ruth 1: 16-17

God saw her faithfulness and conviction to her covenant, and so it pleased Him to move on her behalf. By the time God finished putting her blessings into position, Ruth was married to the man who owned the farm. Not only was Naomi blessed with a grandson to carry her deceased son's name and inheritance, but Ruth became the mother of Obed, the grandmother of Jessie, the great-grandmother of King David and the greaty-greaty-greaty-grandmother of Jesus Christ, Son of God, Prince of Peace, Wonderful Counselor and Rose of Sharon..

Only God can take a poverty stricken person, not to mention an alien in a foreign land, and overnight change their position on earth and in heaven to one of wealth, power and divine legacy.

I'm Just A Man

"So Boaz took Ruth, and she was his wife. And when he went in unto her, she conceived and The Lord gave her a son.

Ruth 4:13

"...Boaz begat Obed, Obed begat Jesse, and Jesse begat David"

Ruth 4:22

Ruth was considered to be a nobody, a broke nobody at that. However, her behavior and steadfastness caught the eye of the master of the land. She was not distracted by the other workers, many of whom were younger men willing to make her promises. Instead she continued to be pleasing to the master. In return, he took her to be his bride and placed her over his household and his servants.

So maybe by today's standards, you too are considered a nobody. You're in luck! God delights in taking anybody who's a nobody, and turning them into somebody sooo great, that everybody has no choice but to give Him the glory.

So go out into the "fields" of your community. Glean those souls not gathered during the harvest. When the bridegroom returns, it will be you He's looking for. So get to work, nobody wants to marry a person stuck in the midst of a personal pity party. That's personally a pitiful excuse!

REFLECT PROCESS & JOURNAL

Write about a situation in your life where you were perceived to be less than who God says you are: _____

_____
_____
_____
_____
_____
_____

Who did you choose to believe: God who created you or the ones who hated you, and why? _____

_____
_____
_____
_____
_____
_____

Talk about the time you felt alone in carrying a weight, with others depending on you. What was the situation & what type of

I'm Just A Man

needs did you have to meet? _____
_____
_____
_____
_____

    When you couldn't physically see another person putting in an effort to help you meet the needs, did you believe that you were, or were not alone and why?_____
_____
_____
_____

    "Trust in Him at all times, O people; pour out your heart before Him; God is a refuge for us. **Selah***"*

Psalm 62:8

    Selah is a musical pause and/or rest, in which all are to listen & meditate. Stop what you are doing and close your eyes. Concentrate on your favorite praise song at a quiet, slow and steady beat. Take

Dr. Casondra R'. Robinson

five or six slow, deep breaths; ten if you are willing to exercise the gift of patience). Now write the feelings and/or thoughts that washed over you: _____

_____

_____

_____

"Blessed is the man...whose delight is in the Law of the LORD, And in His law he meditates day and night. He shall be like a tree Planted by the rivers of water, that bring forth its fruit in its season, Whose leaf also shall not wither; and whatever he does shall prosper."

Psalm 1:1-3

"Finally, breathren, whatever things are true, whatever things are noble, whatever things are just, whatever things are pure, whatever things are lovely, whatever things are of good report, if there is any virtue and if there is anything praiseworthy – meditate on these things. The things which you learned and received and heard and saw in me, these do, and the God of peace will be with you."

Philippians 4:8-9

I'm Just A Man

If you remain loyal to He who became your Father through your marriage to the Bridegroom, He is forever faithful to not only bring you out on the winning side of adversity, but He'll place you in a better, higher place than you started from. Write your thoughts on this: _____

_____
_____
_____
_____
_____
_____
_____
_____
_____
_____
_____
_____

GIDEON

Hello there! We've never met in person, but I'm sure you know someone who would have a few things in common with me. It may even be you who is peeking in my former window, and/or living in my former neighborhood.

I am Gideon, once known as the nobody of nobodies. I come from an unimportant family. We were dirt poor and I was the lowest on the family totem pole. So you can imagine my surprise and disbelief when an angel of The Lord appeared before me.

This holy angel called me a mighty man of valor and proclaimed that The Lord God was with me. Me…Gideon… the lowest of the low, and the weakest of the weak. What could the Almighty Jehovah God want with a loser like me?

Hold on to your sandals folks; He wanted me to free Israel from our oppressors of the last seven years; the mighty Midianites! It had to be a prank, or at the very least, a mistake. After all, how could a God so mighty have faith in me, when I didn't even have faith in myself? And what does Mr. Angel of The Lord have to say about all of this???

"Surely the Lord will be with you and you shall defeat the Midianites

I'm Just A Man

as one man"

Judges 6:16

You know that scripture; *"...greater is He that is in you, than he that is in the world."* Well, it wasn't written until *1 John 4:4*, which came many generations later. So needless to say, I needed some serious convincing!

I began to think up a few test miracles for the angel to perform to ensure this was on the up and up. I prepared a kid goat and unleavened bread deconstructed sandwich and put it in a basket. I saved the broth from the kid in a pot & brought it all before the angel as a sacrifice to The Lord.

"And the angel of God said take the flesh and bread and lay them upon these rocks. Now pour all the broth over it ...Then the angel of the Lord put forth the end of the staff that was in his hand, and touched the flesh and the unleavened cakes; and there rose up fire out of the rock and consumed the flesh and the unleavened cakes. Then the angel of The Lord departed out of his sight."

Judges 6:19-21

Dr. Casondra R'. Robinson

It was then I realized that I had actually seen the face of an angel of The Lord! Man I was scared and started freaking out big time until I heard the voice of The Lord, Himself say:

"Peace be unto thee; fear not; you will not die."

Judges 6:23

Talk about a brother moving quick! I built an altar on that spot and named it "The Lord Is Peace". I was so filled with passion for the Lord that I got together some of my neighborhood crew and tore down my Father's altar to the false god baal, cleared the land around it, built an altar and gave sacrifice to The Lord God Jehovah.

Did I mention the fact that I did all these brave deeds in the middle of the night when everyone was asleep? No? Oh…anyway, talk about some mad folks first thing in the morning!

Now it was on and popping between Jehovah and baal, and I was ready…almost. You see, it's easy to be brave when everyone else is asleep. You can't fault a brother for trying to be really, really, really sure…can you? I talked to The Lord God again, but this time I used my REAL good Hebrew.

I'm Just A Man

"If Thou wilt save Israel by mine hand, as Thou hast said, behold, I will put a fleece of wool in the floor; and if the dew be on the fleece only, and it be dry upon all the earth beside, then shall I know that Thou wilt save Israel by mine hand, as Thou hast said."

Judges 6:36-37

  Pretty fancy huh? You know sometimes when we're not sure how to talk to God, we think it helps to throw in a few thee, thine, thithers and thou's...it can't hurt...right? The next morning the ground was dry and there was enough water in that fleece for me to wring it out in a bowl!

  Soooo okaaay…me…Gideon…slayer of the Midianites. Yep, yep, yep…..that's me alright. Right? Now I didn't want to make God mad but …me…Gideon … slayer of the mighty Midianites… Yep, yep, yep…since you're reading this book anyway, could you just let out a very long sign of confusion & fear for me? Thank you ….I don't feel any better……..but thank you just the same..

Dr. Casondra R'. Robinson

"Let not thine anger be hot against me, and I will speak but this once: let me prove, I pray thee, but this once with the fleece; let it now be dry only upon the fleece and upon all the ground let there be dew."

Judges 6:39

Come morning, it was as I asked, so it looks like I am the instrument chosen to free Israel. I built an army of thirty-two thousand men willing to fight for Israel. I should have checked with God first, because He quickly whittled my army down to a mere three hundred. That meant that we were outnumbered by the Midianites four hundred and fifty to one. If we pull this off with so few men, no one **BUT** the Lord can be praised for the victory.

The Lord sent a dream to the Midianites that they would be defeated by my sword and fear spread though out the camp. That night we stood on the hills surrounding them. When it was time, I gave the signal, we all blew our horns and broke open clay pots with lamps inside.

The Midianites thought they were surrounded and out numbered by a mighty army. When they broke camp, that's just what they did

I'm Just A Man

…broke. All we saw was dust, butts and the bottom of feet as they high-tailed it out of there. I learned something very important that day. When God is on your side, the victory's already won, no matter what the numbers and nay-sayers say. In the beginning, I was very afraid, but I quickly learned I have nothing to fear when I serve the general who kindly reminded me that he didn't even need an army.

So, are you a little nervous about becoming a warrior for the Lord? If so, then take this advice from me; get off your yellow belly, pick up the sword of God, which rest right behind your tongue and get to slaying...starting with your excuse!!!

REFLECT PROCESS & JOURNAL

I'm Just A Man

Write about a situation in your life where you had to fight a battle that you didn't feel confident or equipped to fight: _____
_____
_____
_____
_____
_____
_____
_____

Who did you choose to believe: God who created you or the ones who hated you, and why? _____
_____
_____
_____
_____
_____

Talk about the time you felt alone in carrying a weight, with others depending on you. What was the situation & what type of needs did you have to meet? _____

_____
_____
_____
_____
_____
_____

When you couldn't physically see another person putting in an effort to help you meet the needs, did you believe you were alone, or not and why? _____

_____
_____
_____
_____
_____
_____

Take a moment and read the following eight promises God made to those of us who love Him and are battling evil in every form.

I'm Just A Man

"Because he* loves, me," says the Lord
"I will rescue him'...
I will protect him
for he acknowledges my name
he will call on me
and I will answer him
I will be with him in trouble
I will deliver him
and honor him
With long life I will satisfy him and
show him my salvation."

Psalm 91:14 – 16

*Above, when God says "he" and "him", He means Just A Man named YOU!

You don't have to know the whole bible to be successful in battle. Here's eight promises God makes to those who engage in righteous combat, simply because they love Him. Three verses that say and cover every situation. Write the above promise you want right now and tell why and the outcome you are believing for: _____

_____
_____
_____
_____
_____
_____
_____
_____
_____
_____

Now use what you wrote above, to fill in the following blanks:

Father God I believe you when You said You would _____ me in Psalms 91. I trust You Lord, for You
(Promise)
are He who is eternally faithful. So I surrender control of _____, along with my will, to You. Speak Your
(Circumstance)
plan and will to my heart Lord, and I shall obey in Jesus' name .

I'm Just A Man

Now do us both a huge favor and say "Amen – Amen – Amen" ………wait…….. did you……. nahhhhh… Wait, did you just ...nahhhh….did you just do spiritual warfare? You mean, it's that easy? ….Wow….I guess you **really** don't have an excuse for not thumping on the devil. Ah-Haa! Bwahahahaha!

Now get out there and whoop on that ol' demon some more with that sword on your tongue!

I'M TRYING TO FIND MYSELF

I'm Just A Man

Let's begin with you...stop; look in the mirror ...there you are! See? It's not that hard.....wherever you take yourself; that's where you'll find yourself. Wherever you find yourself; that's exactly where you are. Wherever you are; is exactly where you decided to go or allowed yourself to be lead. Therefore, it's easy to conclude that your problem isn't lack of identity due to lots of confusion. Your problem is lots of "I didn't & not me", due to lack of confession.

You think you've got an identity crisis? Well top this...a murder...dressed like an Egyptian...that was obviously a Hebrew ...educated to rule a nation...but instead a homeless desert vagabond....who found employment as a manny for sheep & goats...with a st-st-st-stutter & a lisssp, named M-M-Moe. How bad is your identity crisis now?   Uhhh huh.....that's what I t-t-thought.

Well, God took Moe and used him to conquer the greatest kingdom of the age with only a crooked stick, faith, flies, frogs (and a few other choice bugs and germs) for ammunition. Then Moe, in one just day, turned a rag-tag group of slaves into a wealthy nation.

So....in the midst of painting yourself blue, hugging a whistling trees, sitting in harmony circles whilst the speaking stick passes and

Dr. Casondra R'. Robinson

the tom-tom pulsates; stand up and speak the following:

>Lord Jesus
>Whatever I am
>However I am
>Here I am
>I am Yours

Now get to work. That swarm of locust just ate your excuse...

"And the daughter of Pharaoh came down to wash herself at the river; and her maidens walked along by the river's side; and when she saw an ark among the flags, she sent her maid to fetch it. And when she opened it, she saw the child: and, behold, the babe wept. And she had compassion on him, and said, 'This is one of the Hebrew's children.'

Then said his sister to Pharaoh's daughter, 'Shall I go and call a nurse of the Hebrew women, that she may nurse the child for thee?' And Pharaoh's daughter said to her, 'Go.' And the maid went and called the child's mother. Pharaoh's daughter said unto her, 'Take this child away

I'm Just A man

and nurse it for me, and I will give thee wages'. And the woman took the child, and nursed it.

And the child grew, and she brought him unto Pharaoh's daughter, and he became her son. And she called his name Moses; and she said, 'Because I drew him out of the water'."

Exodus 2:5-10

Here's a riddle, inside a puzzle, inside a conundrum, inside a question, inside a mystery, inside an enigma: How do you take a Hebrew slave baby, turn him into a prince of Egypt, watch him become a murder and an outcast, present yourself to him from within a burning bush that emits no heat, send him back among the Hebrews as a Midianite sheep herder, and then present him to Pharaoh of Egypt as his long lost royal nephew with all the rights and privileges that come with being the nephew of the richest, most powerful man in the world? You can't, but fortunately for us, God can!

REFLECT PROCESS AND JOURNAL

So, have you been living with multiple purposes and personalities? Are you tired of it? Ready to love what you do and do what you love? Then reflect these reasons why perhaps you are not:

A.   You are living the life that **YOUR** behavior, words and/or plans chose for you

OR

B.   You are living the life that **OTHERS**, through their behavior, words and/or plans, decided you would live.

Did you notice that God is no where in this picture? I personally find that very interesting, since He is the only one with your blueprint. Wise creators always keep the original blueprints to their creations.

And as that He is your creator and the only one with access to your original blueprints, He is the only one who knew the plan for your life before you became a creation.

Want an example? OK – take a raw pot roast and shut it in the trunk of a car in the middle of the summer. Tap the trunk three times with your pointer finger and say "Boop, Boop, Beep – Do your thing microwave!" and walk away for two days. The first hour or so, the roast will appear to be fine, because it is acclimating to its environment. However invisible bacterial is building and the more they builds in numbers, the more it breaks down the roast. Two days later, when you open that steaming trunk, it will be evident that just because you called it a microwave, didn't make it a microwave.

The only way you can function the way you were meant to function, is to be what you were created to be. Who better to show you your purpose, your function, than the One who created you? When God created you, He did so by a divine blueprint that only He possesses.

When God created you, He did so with a plan for your life that He had already put in place. You entered this life only knowing that you were hungry and afraid, but even then you had a purpose, waiting to be fulfilled.

If you want to experience a true and lasting sense of fulfillment, you simply have to fulfill YOUR purpose ~ according to YOUR plan ~ defined in YOUR blueprint ~ by the One who created YOU. Why do you think that after God made you, He broke the mold? Because

I'm Just A Man

when He saw what He'd created in you, He found it to be very good. Just as in the first chapter of Genesis, it is the creation of YOU that makes the good, very good.

Right now, there is probably a Pharisee and Sadducee spirit or two whispering in your ear, "If the mold was broken, then how do you account for identical twins, triplets and quadruplets?".

Well you tell those silly rabbit spirits to try their tricks elsewhere, they already know that this has nothing to do with your exterior housing.

Honey Chile this is not a baby pageant, you are not running for "Grand Supreme" and God is not grading your facial expressions, tap dancing and fashion. Jeremiah 17:10 states that God searches your heart and test your mind ~ the areas where none are identical. Let's do the following test:

<u>Things I Love To Do</u>

The Positive Things	The Negative Things
_____	_____
_____	_____
_____	_____
_____	_____

Dr. Casondra R'. Robinson

_____   _____
_____   _____
_____   _____

The things listed on the negative side, stop it...really...just stop it. Whatever temporary gratification it gives you, is not worth the long term/range cost. List your top three from the positive side and jot down why it rates as such:

1. _____
_____
_____
_____

2. _____
_____
_____
_____

3. _____
_____
_____
_____

I'm Just A Man

You've just listed your purpose for loving what you love, but now consider which one helps others the most...now we are searching for our plan. When you make your life about others, you make the most of YOU.

LIAR LIAR PANTS ON FIRE!

I'm Just A Man

Let's see a show of hands for everyone who knows, that everybody named Abe ain't honest? There's one guy named Abe who was so scared of the owner of a territory he was passing through, he lied and said his fine wife was his good looking sister, and then gave her to the man! *(Genesis 12:10-20)*

Anyone who's never told a lie please stand up. Well…praise the Lord. Take a real good look at the people standing. Those of you with cameras please make sure you take their pictures. Be sure to take your pictures of them with you everywhere you go; show them to your family and friends. That way, they too can know who the *pathological* liars are.

We have all kinds of names for the lies we tell, don't we? Whoppers, tall tales, fabrications, embellishments, verbosity, fibs, fudging, leg pulling, chain jerking, half-truths; not to be confused with stretching the truth, little white lies; not to be mistaken with hugger-muggering, and my very favorite of all; creativeness, just to name a few.

One day, while in the kitchen, I heard a crash that could only be my favorite vase that was so prominently displayed in my living room. Upon entering I saw my four-year old son, <u>the only other</u>

person in the house... standing next to my shattered vase & looking up at me with eyes bigger than my Great-Grandma's Sunday dinner plates.

He immediately began to tell me of the dragon that flew through my closed, locked window and broke my vase just to get him in trouble. And since that mean old dragon tried to get MMYY son in time out, I should find that dragon and put HIM in time out instead. He even offered to help me look for the dragon. I must confess that it took everything I had to keep a straight face; especially when he so diligently helped me look for that mean ol' dragon.

Well, the dragon got off scott-free and so did my son. My family got quite a chuckle that night and we all marveled at his instantaneous *creativeness* in such a dire situation. Then he was four; now he's all grown up and if he tried that same story today he'd be just plain lying, not too old to get stood in a corner and his wages garnished for the cost of my vase. What a difference a day makes!

Maybe you are still creatively verbose. Maybe you are <u>*very*</u> creative. Maybe you are ***extremely*** creative. Take comfort in the fact that you are not alone. I didn't say you were right or justified, only that your misery has plenty of company. Let me tell you about

I'm Just A Man

a fellow we'll call "Pete".

Pete hung out with the group of guys who organized the original Promise Keepers convention.   Their leader was named Immanuel, but we'll call him Manny for Short. Pete was the man to the Main Man. He was big ballin', shot calling and a lot of other terms I'm too darn old to use.

Pete was a big talker and let it be known that that nobody in the group was closer to Manny than him. No one loved Manny more; no one else had Manny's back, according to Pete. Pete & Manny; Manny & Pete, best buds until trouble arose, and then Pete's feet got fleet!

Well, one night Manny had trouble that started out looking like a situation. Some fellows, jealous of Manny's successful ministry came up to them, acting like they were ready to make some furniture move. That was a situation and Pete jumped up and cut off the ear of the guy nearest to him. Pete was ready to rumble… unfortunately the rabble rousers brought the cops with them. That was not a situation…that was trouble & suddenly Pete's heard his mother calling him home.

Folks began to call him out as one of the main men in Manny's crew; whereas he promptly cursed them out. He watched Manny get smacked around, all the while swearing they'd never met. Let's hear what Pete has to say for himself:

"I have Intermittent Explosive Behavior Disorder aka IEBD in the psychiatric world. A more common name for it is a "Hair Trigger Temper". I know I'm saved through Christ. I walked with Manny for three years, but in certain situations I would just lose it. In spite of my high position in the church, I would curse you out in a heartbeat, not to mention I had no problem cutting off your ear and waiting for Jesus to put it back on.

But my greatest sin, the worse thing I ever did, the thing that I am most ashamed of; is when Manny needed me the most…I denied Him. Not just once, but THREE times. Fortunately, He had mercy on my soul and granted me redemption, even from my greatest sin, and then commissioned me to care for his people."

"…Jesus said to Simon Peter,"Simon, son of Johan, do you love me more than all my other disciples?"" Peter answered ""Yes Lord; you

I'm Just A Man

know that I love you." Jesus said "then feed my sheep". (That's one denial down and two to go). Jesus said to him again, the second time "Simon, son of Jonah, do you love me?" Peter answered "Yes Lord; you know that I love you". Jesus said "then feed my sheep" Jesus spoke to him a third time "Simon, son of Jonah, do you love me?" Peter was grieved because Jesus asked him a third time if he truly loved Him. He said "Lord, you know all things; you know that I love you" Jesus said "Feed my sheep."

John 21:15-17

"I was among the first filled with His Holy Spirit."

"Then Jesus said to them ""Peace be unto you.: as my Father sent me, I am now sending you."" And when He said this, He breathed on them saying ""receive the Holy Ghost within you. Whomsoever's sins you forgive, they are truly forgiven and whomsoever's sins you condemn, they are truly condemned""."

John 20: 21-23

Dr. Casondra R'. Robinson

"I received a new ministry of signs and wonders."

"And by the hands of the apostles were many signs and wonders done among the people (and they were all with one accord in Solomon's porch. And of the rest dared no man join himself to them, but the people esteemed them highly. And more believers were added to The Lord, multitudes of both men and women) So much so, that they brought the sick into the streets and laid them on beds and couches, that at the least the shadow of Peter passing by might land on some of them. There came also a multitude out of the cities surrounding Jerusalem, bringing sick people, and those who were possessed with demonic spirits: and they were healed, each and every one."

Acts 5:12-16

"I began the Judeo-Christian church at the house of Cornelius, a Roman centurion."

"Then Peter opened his mouth and said, Of a truth I perceive that God is (impartial) no respecter of people, but in every nation he that fears Him

and works in righteousness is accepted with Him.

The word which God sent unto the children of Israel, preaching peace by Jesus Christ: (He is Lord of all:) That word, I say, you know which was proclaimed throughout all Judea, and began from Galilee, after the baptism which John preached; How God anointed Jesus of Nazareth with the Holy Ghost and with power: who went about doing good and healing all that were oppressed of the devil; for God was with Him.

And we are witnesses of all things which he did both in the land of the Jews and in Jerusalem; whom they murdered and hanged on a tree: Him God raised up the third day, and showed Him openly; Not to all the people, but unto witnesses chosen before of God, even to us, who did eat and drink with Him after He rose from the dead.

And He commanded us to preach unto the people, and to testify that it is He which was ordained of God to be the Judge of quick and dead. To Him give all the prophets witness, that through His name whosoever believes in Him shall receive forgiveness of sins. While Peter yet spoke these words, The Holy Ghost fell on all them which heard the word. And they of the circumcision (The Jews) which believed were astonished, as many as came with Peter, because that on the Gentiles also was poured out the gift of The Holy Ghost. For they heard them speak with tongues, and magnify God.

Then answered Peter, can any man forbid water that these should not be baptized, which have received The Holy Ghost the same as we?

And he commanded them to be baptized in the name of The Lord..."

Acts 10: 34-38

"I was a liar and a denier. I repented and became an Apostle of Holy Fire."

Simon Peter

You been telling lies lately? Well repent and go forth speaking the truth of Christ's Passion. If you're trying to use your past behavior as an excuse, I know and you know, that you just lied again: SO STOP IT and get about His business!!!

REFLECT PROCESS AND JOURNAL

Dr. Casondra R'. Robinson

Soooooo....are you also a hugger-mugger? Have you been stretching the truth...just a little bit? You're not the first and won't be the last. The question is, what are you going to do about it today? List below three whoppers you've told, that you would take back if you could.

1. _____

2. _____

3. _____

Are any of the above lies as bad as Abe's or Pete's? I seriously doubt it, especially Pete's. Not that they may prove to be more inconvenient for you, seeing as how they did come from behind *Your* front teeth, but in the grand scheme of the world, no. Just as they repented, you need to also repent. If you're not sure how, just repeat the following aloud:

I'm Just A Man

Father God, I come before You
Seeking forgiveness for my behavior
Though there is joy in Your presence
My heart is full of remorse and sorrow
I'm a liar
I knew I was wrong
But it felt right and was easier to lie,
Than to tell the truth
I'm tired of maneuvering around the lies
I'm tired of giving honor to the father of lies
Strengthen me,
Free me of this behavior,
My heart is convicted
I release the burden of my behavior to You
Cleanse me right now
Receive me as I am
In Jesus' name – Amen – Amen – Amen

Congratulations on your release! Now you have to move quickly, the opportunity to lie again will come sooner that you think, because the devil now wants to test your resolve.

Have you ever heard the statement that knowledge is power? Well...we both have knowledge of the fact that you were just recently a liar. We both have knowledge of the fact that at this moment, you are not a liar. What we don't have knowledge of, is what was that feeling?

The feeling I mean, is the one brought to the surface by the situation you were in, that caused you to lie, rather than deal with the truth of those emotions.

Unmalicious and/or self-serving lies usually stem from feelings of inadequacy or inferiority. If you are having these feelings, it means that you judge yourself by man's standards and who he says you are.

But remember, that's the same man who did not create you, that's the same man who can not save you, that's the same man who does not unconditionally love you, taking you as you are and that's the same man who has no place to put you when this life is over.

So let's look at and then journal about some of the things that the One who did all those things for you, has to say about you. I'll give you the scripture and you fill in the blanks.

I'm Just A Man

You Are Beautiful Because You Are Made In The Very Image Of God

Genesis 5:1 _____

_____

_____

_____

You Are Not God's Heir By Coincidence, He Chose You

Ephesians 1:4-5 _____

_____

_____

_____

He Doesn't Hold Your Past Against You

2 Corinthians 5:19 _____

_____

_____

_____

Dr. Casondra R'. Robinson

You Were Smart Enough To Repent, So You're Smarter Than Most

Job 28:28 _____

_____

_____

_____

He Declares You Are Brave

Psalm 27:1 _____

_____

_____

_____

You Can Operate In Success

Philippians 4:13 _____

_____

_____

_____

I'm Just A Man

So tap into the you, that you were created to be and if anyone tries to give you a reason as to why you should not serve God...guess what? *They lying*!!! (Sometimes improper English is necessary, so stop judging me!). PS – If your lies were malicious: A) **STOP BEING SO DAG GUMM PETTY!** B) repent   C) Devote that time to getting busy for the cause of the Lord!

I
HAVE
A
"DIS"-ABILITY

I'm Just A Man

"And Moses said unto the Lord, O my Lord, I am not eloquent, neither heretofore, nor since thou hast spoken unto thy servant; but I am slow of speech and of a slow tongue.

And the Lord said unto him, Who hath made man's mouth? Or who makes the dumb or deaf, or the seeing, or the blind? Have not I, The Lord? Now therefore go, and I will be with thy mouth and teach thee what thou shall say."

Exodus 4:10-12

I 'm not very good with words, I also stutter and have a lisp. But God used me to turn poverty ridden slaves, into the wealthy nation of Israel in just one day. I didn't walk on water, but through the power of God, I parted a sea right down the middle so His people could cross on bone dry land. When our enemies tried to follow us, the power of The Lord was upon me and the waters closed so that none of them would live to ever follow us again.

God used me to feed His people, heal His people, instruct His people, protect His people and teach His people to defend themselves. Me, a nobody. I was born a slave, raised a false prince, cast out as a murderer and lived forty years as a shepherd of sheep that weren't even my own. Now…add the stutter AND the lisp… welcome to my world. Got a hard luck story? How about an obvious disability? Then God will get more glory from you, than from the "normal" people! Now stop critiquing yourself in the world's fun house mirror and get to work!

Moe aka Mosheh aka Moses

I was known as God's Prophet. But there was something about me unknown, I suffered from clinical depression. I was suicidal and even prayed to God to die.

"But he himself went a day's journey into the wilderness, and came and sat down under a juniper tree: and he requested for himself that he might die; and said, it is enough; now O Lord take away my life, for I am not better than my fathers".

1 Kings 19:4

Instead God sent an angel to comfort and sustain me. I became an even greater prophet and performed miracles though God that brought down a corrupt kingdom, destroyed a false religion, its false prophets and helped Israel find their way back to God. When my work was done, God still wouldn't let me die. Instead He sent a hot rod that was literally aflame, to personally pick me up and carry me straight into His presence.

"...Behold, there appeared a chariot of fire, and parted them asunder; and Elijah went up by a whirlwind into heaven. And Elisha saw it, and he cried my father, my father, the chariot of Israel, and the horsemen thereof. And he saw him no more.

2 Kings 2:11-12

"...for the Joy of the Lord is your strength".

Nehemiah 8:10

Ever notice how depression and exhaustion seem to go hand in hand? Curse your depression in Jesus' name...make yourself, dance yourself right into joy…and then laugh away your excuse and merrily get to work!

Elijah the Tishbite

REFLECT PROCESS AND JOURNAL

Are you using a disability as an excuse not to participate in God's plan for your life. Before you are quick to say no, claims of inability due to disability is lowest among the physically disabled. We'll come back to this, but first let's consider other forms of disability.

MENTAL DISABILITY

THE CLINICALLY DIAGNOSED:

So let's deal with the obvious, if you have a clinical diagnoses, chances are you also have medication and/or therapy. If you are not taking your medications and/or attending your sessions, I need you to correct that behavior immediately. All wisdom, understanding and knowledge comes from God, the key word here being **ALL**.

Whatever medical knowledge your doctor has, it was God who gave the ability to acquire, process and maintain it. You can't base your obedience on your doctor's faith, personal choices, beliefs, nor their place of origin. You can't base it on the doctor at all – you must base it on the word; and the word says that the knowledge they have, comes from God whether they acknowledge it or not.

Have you ever considered that the doctor's purpose for being there, was to provide you with the medical care you needed? Whether or not the doctor *intended* to follow God's plan, as Christians we know that God always has a plan, and HE often uses those out of His will ~ to bring His will to pass.

Do not base your obedience on self-diagnosis. That you feel fine and have not had a recent crisis, is not an excuse. The prescribed treatment is usually to ensure that you not get stable, but *stay* stable. Once you are set in the stability position, God can use you more, take your further and position you higher. So follow the doctor's orders and continue to read this book; Your present excuse, just became your past excuse and we have work to do.

THE MENTALLY CHALLENGED:

I said challenged, not delayed, so don't get it twisted. Because God is who He is - He cares for us the way He does and it is His nature to constantly challenge us. He doesn't do it to make us feel inferior, but so that we grow in faith. We learn that through Him we are undefeatable in all we set our hand to, when we move according to His will.

How many times has an opportunity presented itself and because you doubted your own ability to perform the task, you closed the door to it? How many times has God given you the ideal of a business or a book that you did not pursue? How long did it take for you to discover that what you wouldn't do, someone else later did and now they possess the benefits that would have been yours, if only you would had been obedient?

The Father does not give us task which we are incapable of accomplishing, but He does make a habit of giving us task which we have yet to accomplish. All good parents nurture, develop, grow and strengthen the abilities of their offspring. We all want our children to be able to obtain and maintain multiple avenues of blessings that will sustain and increase them.

Does it therefore make any sense that God would be different? What form of reasoning leads you to believe that we mortal parents, could possibly parent better than the One who created parenting?

I was not the perfect parent, but on many occasions told my children, "You can accomplish your goal because you are mine. You may falter at times, but **I will** catch you before you fall." When my children address me, they say Mama, Mom or in the case of my son,

Mother. But with all of them, the name they call me when trouble arises is "Mommy". All are grown, some are married and I am a grandmother six times over; but you better believe that when I hear my nurture name "Mommy", my battle gear goes on and I am ready to **SLAY** whomever it is...whatever it is...that is causing my child distress.

   I don't care where on this planet my babies are, it matters not the depth of the problem they are experiencing; they just gave the problem to Mommy and now the one(s) with the problem ~ are the ones that upset my babies; my very grown, but still very much mine, babies.

   Can you imagine how much more fierce Your Holy Father is concerning you? Your all seeing, all knowing and ever present Father will always be ever protectively moving for His beloved children. Did you know that He also has a name that can be used by His children who are filled with self-doubt.

   When I hear those emotional barriers in my head that say I am too weak, too small, too uneducated, too lowly or unimportant to get things accomplished, I call on my Father, Jehovah-Shamah. It means "The Lord Is There". I call on the Parent who will never

I'm Just A Man

leaves me to my feelings of low self-esteem, but who instead will encourage me, saying "You can accomplish your goal because you are Mine. You may falter at times, but **I will** catch you before you fall."

Write below the ideas that God has given, which you have refused to accept as your task. Pray to Jehovah-Shamah and thank Him for being with you as you undertake this challenge. Then ask Jehovah-Jireh, Divine Provider, to provide you with the knowledge to succeed; and Jehovah-Shalom, Divine Peace, to take away your doubts and fears, replacing them with trust and peace.

Father God In Jesus' Name: _____

_____
_____
_____
_____
_____
_____
_____

Dr. Casondra R'. Robinson

_____
_____
_____
_____
_____

"For God has not given us a spirit of fear, but of power and of love and of a sound mind."

2 Timothy 1:7

EMOTIONAL DISABILITY

No one enters into the world depressed. When we a young all things are possible – unicorns and dragons are real, we can tie a bath towel around our neck and fly; life has no limits until someone whose word we trust, tells us different.

Depression happens as we travel life's path, not surrounded by positive people during the times when we need encouragement. Maybe you've been surrounded by nay-sayers, those who go out of their way to speak against your every hope and dream. I've been there. Maybe you've been surrounded by those who looked your way, but never saw you; instead they saw someone related to you, whom they hated. They couldn't punish that person, so they took it out on you instead. I've been there too.

Perhaps no one has ever discouraged you, but there was a time when you fell and no one encouraged you to get back up and try again. You decided it was easier and safer to just lay there, and so you stayed.

It could have been that you did not have the knowledge of God, to have the necessary faith in Him to aid you. It could have been that you had the knowledge, but lacked the faith. Whatever the reason, it's important that you know that not only does the Lord think of you, but His thoughts of you are peaceful, positive and full of hope.

"For I know the thoughts that I think toward you, says the Lord, thoughts of peace and not of evil, to give you a future and a hope."

Jeremiah 29:11

Below, write down your honest emotional beliefs concerning your purpose and plan today. Even if you are not under distress, write them down.

Concerning my ability to fulfill God's plan for my life, I feel:

_____
_____
_____
_____
_____
_____
_____
_____

Now write a prayer telling God how you feel right now, and how you **want** to be able to feel about yourself and your abilities. Ask Him to help you release the pain and doubt, but hold on to the lessons learned. Let it all go in prayer and speak into existence the person you want your future emotional self to be. Set aside a time to say this prayer everyday, for thirty days.

I'm Just A Man

Father God In Jesus' Name: _____

_____
_____
_____
_____
_____
_____
_____
_____
_____
_____

At the end of thirty days, write down your honest emotional beliefs concerning your purpose and plan. Compare it to the first time you wrote it, acknowledging that any sign of change is progress, and you **will** see a change after thirty days of sincere prayer.

Dr. Casondra R'. Robinson

Concerning my ability to fulfill God's plan for my life, I feel:

_____
_____
_____
_____
_____
_____
_____

PHYSICAL DISABILITY

Physical disabilities do not disable your ability to fulfill your Destiny, or to share the gospel………..period….... Next chapter please!

MY PAST
WON'T LET
ME HAVE
A FUTURE

I'm Just A Man

So…you think that your past mistakes have destroyed your hopes of a decent future do you? First of all; remember that anyone pointing a finger at you, has three fingers pointing back at them. There is no shame in starting over. Even Jesus Christ had to leave His home town to fulfill the destiny God had for him. The people couldn't see who God had created Him to be, because they were stuck on the Him that He used to be. They constantly spoke of His family, who He was back in the day. Therefore they could not receive Him for who He was in their here and now.

"And He went out from thence, and came into His own country; and His disciples followed Him. And when the Sabbath day was come, Jesus began to teach in the synagogue: And many hearing Him were astonished, saying from whence hath this man these things? And what wisdom is this which is given unto Him, that even such mighty works a wrought by His hands. Is this not the carpenter, the son of Mary, the brother of James, and Joses, and of Judah and Simon? And are not His sisters here with us? And they were offended at Him.

But Jesus said unto them, "A prophet is not without honor, but in his

I'm Just A Man

own county, and among his own kin, and in his own house." And He could there do no mighty work, save that He laid His hands upon a few sick folk, and healed them. And He marveled because of their unbelief. And He went round about the villages, teaching.

Mark 6:1-6

Sometimes you must change your surroundings and associates to match the person you are striving to become. BOOM!....That was just me blowing up you excuse!

REFLECT PROCESS AND JOURNAL

I'm Just A Man

Everybody has a Pookie, Re-Re and the gang in their lives. Those are the people who use passive-aggressive tactics to try to make you feel bad that you have progressed in your life. If you are familiar with these people, finish these statements:

"Awww you ain't nobody! I remember when you used to: _____
_____"

"Awww you ain't nobody! I remember when you didn't have: __
_____"

"Awww you ain't nobody! I remember when you used to be the first one to: _____
_____"

Does writing these statements about who you were then, change who God has grown you to become now? Of course not; you've been so focused on the better God is leading you to, that you haven't used your valuable time to meditate on that long gone thing – no more so than a college graduate crossing the stage is focused on their first day of kindergarten.

THE TRUTH ABOUT POOKIE, RE-RE & THE GANG

1) That place you graduated from, they're still there

2) They chose not to do the work you did to advance, but instead to sit down and blame everyone and everything for their stagnation

3) By calling someone on a higher level a nobody, it allows them a brief moment to pretend that their choice to be stagnant, still makes them better than you

4) It angers them that in their misery, you could be happy

5) Instead of confessing and addressing their part in their misery, they find it easier to blame you and "those like you", as the reason for their misery

5) Misery loves company

I'm Just A Man

A FEW POSSIBLE RESPONSES

1. "All the more reason I thank God for growing me; but hey... enough about me...tell me the wonderful ways that you've grown"

2. "I can't imagine how sad my life would be if **I** chose not to walk away and follow God"

3. "Yes, thank God I learned that the closer I get to Him, the higher He'll take me"

These responses all give you an opportunity to witness on the benefits of following Christ without preaching, but instead just responding. Although you used yourself in each statement, the real statement made is about the life of the stagnant person.

Finally, each statement blocks the enemy's opportunity to make you speak regret over God's blessings and love towards you. It blocks you from feeling anger or shame over an issue falsely placed on your shoulders. It reminds you that you have nothing to prove to satan, nor his snaggle-tooth employees.

And do you know why his employees are all snaggle-toothed? Because it's the only way they can stick that forked tongue out and taste the air for signs of meals made of the doubt and shame of others. Find a response that is sweet, but with an edge so sharp, it can easily behead that thing.

I'M A PERSON OF ILL REPUTE

Dr. Casondra R'. Robinson

RAHAB'S CONFESSION

I'm not ashamed to admit it; I was a chickenhead. Yep, I was a straight-up ho. But hey, I had no man, bills were due, I just did what I felt I had to do. It paid a lot better than begging or government assistance. Sometimes I wanted to go to church, but I didn't. It seemed to make everybody nervous. The wives thought I wanted their husbands & the husbands thought I might bust them out, but that would have been the fun part. In truth, I stayed away because I didn't feel like being judged by folks who acted as if they didn't have a past or a right now, for that matter.

Then I met these two guys from out of town who served a different God. They and their God, were the opposite of everything sacred that I was familiar with, especially the preachers I ***"knew,"*** knew. They talked to me with respect and kindness. They talked to me as if I mattered. Turns out they were spies; soldiers of this God I didn't know. And because of how they treated me, I found myself wanting to know the God they served.

They warned me of coming destruction. Even my city's gods, priest and priestesses would not be spared. But me…a ho…an unworthy soul by anyone's standard, would be spared. All I had to do, was be obedient to the instructions of these men concerning the word God gave them.

That one act of obedience saved not only my life; but the lives of my family and all that we had. For the first time, in a very long time, I am truly alive and at peace in my spirit. It's a gift that I can never repay. Glory to The God Of Israel, He who spares and adopts any who would but put their trust in Him!

Now I'm no fool; I know there will always be some church folks out there who will never let me, nor anyone else forget my past. They're gonna gossip about me, act funky, try to make me feel ashamed and throw it in my face every chance that they get. But if only they knew...I never...ever... want to forget my past; remembering it makes my present sweeter. Acknowledging my past darkness, makes my future destiny just that much brighter.

Are you now, or have you ever been a whore; a chickenhead, a trollop, a gigolo, a player-player, a skank, a scrub, a lady's man, a jezebel, a home wrecker, or a Jody? Have you ever, with your married self, partaken of the services of one? That's no excuse, get a penicillin shot, pray to the God of Israel for forgiveness, forgive yourself, shake the dust from your feet and get to work.

" ...Now therefore, I pray you, swear unto me by The LORD, since I have shown you kindness (for fear and respect of your God), that you will also show kindness unto my father's house, and give me a true token. And that you will save alive my father, and my mother, and my brothers, and my sisters, and all that they have, and deliver us from death. And the men answered her, Our life is yours, if you utter not this our business. And it shall be, when The Lord hath given us the land, that we will deal kindly and truly with thee."

Joshua 2:12-14

BALLAM'S CONFESSION

I was a self-made (and self-proclaimed) pagan prophet for sale; a well known soothsayer, psychic, seer of the unseen and diviner of the unknown. Having a head for business, I used my gift to my advantage. I'd made the surrounding pagan religions my business

I'm Just A Man

and believe me when I say that business was GOOD!

Kings would ask me to prophesy prosperity to their people and curses upon their enemies. I would gladly fulfill the king's request, then go to his enemy and do the same. I call myself an entrepreneur who had an "understanding" with his clients. Today people might say I played on both sides of the fence or maybe even call me the king of kickbacks.

But one day, things changed; Balak, king of Moab, sent the elders of Moab and Midian with a bag of money (my usual fee) and asked me to curse the people of Israel. I invited them to spend the night & then come morning we would go. I would put on a show worth the money they were paying me. But...that night while I slept, God warned me not to conduct my business as usual concerning these particular people.

God said to me "Do not go with these men. You shall not curse the people of Israel, for I have blessed them."

Numbers 22:12

Dr. Casondra R'. Robinson

Now I ain't nobody's fool, so I sent the elders back home, telling them The God of Israel had restrained me. I was known to be a good negotiator, so it was no surprise when the king sent his princes to entreat me with more wealth, high position and any other desire of my heart. JACKPOT! You better believe that I was up bright and early, riding high and mighty on my ass, ready to do business.

Picture it…there I was….riding down the road...surrounded by princes no less...when my ass turned off the road and went into a field. I beat her until she returned to the road.

Then she pushed herself up against a wall, crushing my foot in the process. I beat that ass again, trying to hide my embarrassment at my own ass' behavior.

Then she just fell out on the ground and refused to budge. I took my staff and beat the stuffing out of my ass. After all, I was Ballam the great seer and no dumb ass was going to make a dumb ass of me, especially in front of such prestigious clientele.

Okay…now I know there are many religious leaders who partake of certain liquids and herbs so that they can see things unseen to others. But trust me, I was not drunk, high nor tweaking when this happened…..my – ass – started – talking – to – me! I was so shocked that I answered without thinking. I was having a conversation...with my own ass! It went a little something like this:

ASS: *"What have I done to you to make you beat me three times?"*

ME: *"Because you have made me look stupid. I wish I had a sword in my hand so I could kill you!"*

ASS: *"Am I not your very own ass? The same ass you've ridden since you first bought me? Have I ever been guilty of making you look stupid before?"*

ME: *"No..."*

Numbers 22:28-30

Suddenly, there stood an angel of The Lord before me with his sword drawn for battle. In fear, I immediately fell flat on my face.

Now if you thought that last conversation was interesting, wait until you hear about my confabulation with the angel of The Lord!

Dr. Casondra R'. Robinson

ANGEL: "Why have you whipped your own ass three times? I stood here as the adversary who would take your life, because your ways are contrary to the way of The Lord. Your ass saw me and three times turned you from my sword. If it were not for your ass, you would be dead and yet I would have let your ass live."

ME (sniveling): "I have sinned; I didn't know that you were sent to kill me for my rebellion. If it will save my life, I'll just mosey on home now....."

ANGEL: "No! You wanted to go with the princes, so you just mosey on with them. BUT, when it is time for you to prophesy, speak only the words I will give you.

Numbers 22:32-35

Now what this was going to do for my profitable business of custom ordered prophecies, which included perks and kickbacks, along with my usual fee, I didn't know. I went and met with King

I'm Just A Man

Balak, my current client. He gave me above my usual fee, so with great pomp, I set up my seven altars, did my usual sacrifices, yada, yada, yada...I had a problem. Even though I was hired to curse Israel, every time I opened my mouth, I could only speak blessings. Needless to say, my clients were not happy. God had used them to bless Israel when their true intent was to curse and destroy them. I could not reverse what God had said or done. I kept trying to accommodate my client, but again and again and again I could only speak blessings.

King Balak finally said he would rather that I simply not speak at all, but God had my tongue and there was nothing I could do but speak even greater blessings upon Israel.

"God is not a man, therefore He does not lie. Neither is He born of man, therefore He is not wont to change His mind. If He said it, He shall do it; if He speaks it, He shall make it so".

Numbers 23: 19

I learned four very important things that day…

Dr. Casondra R'. Robinson

1) The Lord God will protect with a vengeance those whom He loves

2) The Lord God uses the enemies who would curse His people, to bless them greatly

3) Live your life contrary to The Lord God's will long enough, and you'll end up beating your own ass

4) It is better to let the words of God come from your own mouth, rather than your own ass!

Stop being an ass, get up off your excuse and give God control of your tongue, your actions and your life. Now!

REFLECT PROCESS AND JOURNAL

Dr. Casondra R'. Robinson

Are you letting the fact that you have an illicit past, keep you from having a future? OK, I've been stuck there before, so let's talk about it. We'll start by listing up to 5 illicit things that you have done:

1. _____

2. _____

3. _____

4. _____

5. _____

Now pick just one of the five above to write below, BUT ONLY if it's a sin never committed by anyone ever, in the history of the whole wide world....

1. _____

What?....You had nothing wickedly new to offer us?....All right, all right...cool, cool, cool…....lets try another one from a different direction: pick one of the five sinful acts you listed above and write it below, BUT ONLY if God is incapable of forgiving it.

1. _____

OK...I missed it...why don't you have a future? That's what I thought! The only thing wrong with you, is you need to realize that you're at a different type of party with a much better DJ, music and refreshments. Grab hold to your new dance partner, work your holy dance and leave your pity party state of mind. It's time to get on the floor and bust a move for God!

I HAVE A CRIMINAL RECORD

Dr. Casondra R'. Robinson

JAKE'S STORY

Everyone thinks it's just sooo sweet when children are baptized. No one is surprised when a goody-two-shoes gets dipped. But when the black sheep of the family...the trouble maker...the thief...the skeezer...the con artist...the rabble rouser...the alcoholic...the drug addict...the one that "ain't never gonna amount to nothing"...that one guaranteed to have a staring role on a future episode of "Cops" or "First 48" gets saved; it causes an outbreak of salvation.

Family members that have strayed from their faith, rededicate their lives. Those who have never had a relationship with God, will seek to develop one. Ray Ray and Bubba's old crew may be calling him soft, but some of them secretly would love to live without having to look over their shoulder every couple of minutes. If you pay attention, every now and then, a few will pull him aside and ask a lot of "hypothetical" questions.

When a super sinner, one of the devil's best buddies, gets saved, it gets a lot of attention. Household, families and even communities can be changed by one super sinner's surrender to Christ. There was this con-artist and thief named Jake; a real mama's boy that would

I'm Just A Man

steal from his own kin if you didn't watch him. Actually, he did steal from his family; he took his older brother's blessing and inheritance during a weak moment and then tricked his blind daddy into notarizing it, thus making it binding.

Talk about low down. His mama, Becky, who favored him over his brother and helped him trick his daddy, was no better. You'd better believe that after his brother discovered his dastardly deed, Jake had to get out of Dodge and fast. His brother swore he'd kill him, so Becky schemed to get him on the first camel out of town.

She went to Jake's daddy, acting all sad about the fact that there were no nice Jewish girls in the neighborhood. Oy vey! They were surrounded by those Canaanite floozies, who were loose and worshiped false gods. How could she go to her grave in peace having grandchildren by the likes of them?

However, praise be to God, she had a solution to this humongous problem. She just "happened" to remember that her brother, Haran, had daughters who could give them many grandchildren raised according to their Hebrew tradition. By the time she was through acting all pitiful, Isaac thought it was his idea and told Jake to get to getting to Haran's house. On the way there, Jake pulled over at a rock to get a good night's sleep.

"And he dreamed, and saw a ladder set up on the earth, and the top of it reached to heaven; and he saw the angels of God climbing up and down the ladder. ...the Lord stood above it and said "I am the Lord God of Abraham thy father, and the God of Isaac; the land where you are lying I will give it to you and your descendants.

And your descendants shall be as numerous as the dust of the earth and you shall spread abroad to the west, east, north and south and in you and your descendants shall all the families of the earth be blessed...I am with you and will keep you in all places wherever you go and will bring you again into this land; for I will not leave you until I have done that which I have spoken to you."

Genesis 28:11-15

I'm Just A Man

You see, it was God's plan all along for Jake to receive this blessing. He didn't have to steal it, he only had to be patient and wait for The Lord to move on his behalf. But nooooooo! Like so many of us, rather than wait:

> We want what we want
> Like we want it
> How we want it
> And when we want it
> Which is usually right now!

God's plan for each of our lives is unchanging. It is our obedience or disobedience that determines its timing and fruition. God's plan for him will come to pass, but Jake will have to deal with the consequences of his decisions first.

Now after Becky helped him dupe his daddy and split out of town, you'd think Jake would have watched his uncle (her brother for goodness sakes!) for any signs of the family trait of trickery. But once again; noooooooooooo, our boy had to learn the hard way that you reap what you sow. And WOW was he gonna sow it good, because his uncle Haran had been at this game longer than Jake had been alive!

His uncle had this gorgeous daughter named Rachel. When Jake laid eyes on her, he knew it was time to turn in his player card. Haran made Jake an offer he couldn't refuse; stay with him and help raise his livestock (without pay) and in seven years the wedding could commence. With no negotiation, Jake said "sounds good to me" (dummy) and went to work. Those seven years were good for Haran, because he understood that Jake was blessed, which made his flocks and herds multiply greatly.

Have you ever heard the saying that "Love is blind"? Well in Jake's case love was not only blind, but crippled, crazy and afflicted to boot. So much so, that seven long years seemed like only a few days, until it was his long awaited payday. Now he would marry his beautiful and beloved Rachel.

The wedding was fantastic! One of the traditions of a wedding is that of the bride wearing a veil. Have you ever wondered why she wears that little thin….wispy….see through piece of fabric? Because

I'm Just A Man

of Jacob: you see boys and girls, his wife was brought to him with a beautiful (not to mention thick) veil covering her face. The ceremony was complete, everyone danced and cheered for the happy couple.

Then finally it was just Jake and his wife, alone in a very, very dark tent. Can I get someone to testify that darkness is always followed by the light of day? Well, what followed the next morning was the discovery that he was married to Leah, Rachel's older and much plainer sister....which is why brides now wear transparent veils...you want to KNOW FOR SURE that the one walking down the aisle, is the one you actually agreed to marry! How dare his Uncle trick him out of something that was rightfully his! Really Jake? This don't sound the *least* bit familiar to you?...Really???

Jake married Rachel a week later, but it cost him another seven years of servitude and ten "adjustments" in his salary. Now he's stuck with two wives, one whom he loves, one he does not and each one knew, which one she was.

We have a new word today boys and girls, can you say "**D R A M A**"? That's the word we'll use to describe Jake's household. As a matter of fact, by the time he came into his destiny, he had FOUR wives, only one whom he loved. Can you say "**BABY MAMA DRAMA**" boy's and girls? Jake went through more than twenty years of the soap opera lifestyle before coming into his destiny: all because he decided to get what he wanted by crooked means.

Like Jake, many of us make mistakes, some which leave us to carry a criminal record for the rest of our lives. But it doesn't mean that your life is over. God can take a criminal, change his or her heart, even change what people call them, make them fruitful and blessed beyond what their minds can imagine.

That's what God did for Jake. He went from being called thief and con man to Prince with God, or as it's more commonly known "Israel".

Yep, that's our Jake; Israel, father of the twelve tribes of Israel; progenator of the Jewish nation; forefather of the Judeo-Christian faith through one of his descendants; Jesus Christ – maybe you've heard of him.

Now before you dwell on your particular crime, meditate on a few facts proving that God has a purposeful plan for everyone, and can make big things out of those who see themselves as among the least.

I'm Just A Man

King David's Story of Sex, Lies & Murder

"...David arose from off his bed, and walked upon the roof of the king's house: and from the roof he saw a woman bathing herself, and the woman was very beautiful to look at. And David sent and inquired after the woman. And one said ""Is not this Bathsheba, the daughter of Eliam, the wife of Uriah the Hittite?"" And David sent messengers, and took her; and she came in to him and he lay with her; for she was purified from her uncleanness; and she returned unto her house. And the woman conceived and sent and told David, and said I am with child."

2 Samuel 11:2-5

"...David wrote a letter to Joab and sent it by Uriah. And he wrote in the letter, saying, Set Uriah in the forefront of the fiercest battle, and then pull back from him, that he may be struck down and die.

And it came to pass, when Joab observed the city, that he assigned Uriah unto a place where he knew that valiant warriors were. And the men of the city went out, and found with Joab, and there fell some of the people of the servants of David; and Uriah the Hittite died also."

2 Samuel 11:15-17

Saint Peter Had A Violent And Potentially Deadly Temper

"Then He asked them again, ""Who are you looking for?"" and they said, Jesus of Nazareth. Jesus answered, ""I have told you that I am He; if you are looking for only me, then let these others go their own way: that the saying might be fulfilled, which He had said, ""Of them which you gave me I have lost none."" Then Simon Peter having a sword drew it, and struck the high priest's servant, and cut off his right ear. The servant's name was Malchus.

Then Jesus said to Peter ""Put your sword back into it's sheath; Shall I not drink the cup which my Father has given me (fulfill my purpose)?   *John 18:7-11*

I'm Just A Man

Moses: A Killer Who Lived Life On The Lam For Forty Years

"And it came to pass in those days, when Moses was grown, that he went out unto his brethren, (the Hebrews) and looked on their burdens: and he saw an Egyptian beating a Hebrew, one of his brethren. And he looked this way and that way, and when he saw that there was no man, he murdered the Egyptian and hid him in the sand."
Exodus 2:11-12

"Now when Pharaoh heard this thing, he sought to kill Moses. But Moses fled from the face of Pharaoh, and dwelt in the land of Midian..."
Exodus 2:15

Before Saul Became Paul

"...When they heard these things, they were cut to the heart and began to bite Stephen with their teeth. But he, being full of The Holy

Stephen looked up steadfastly into heaven and saw the glory of God, and Jesus standing on the right hand of God. And said "Behold, I see the heavens opened, and the Son of Man standing on the right hand of God".

Then they cried out with a loud voice and stopped their ears, and ran upon him with one accord. And cast him out of the city, and stoned him; and the witnesses laid down their clothes at a young man's feet, whose name was Saul.

And they stoned Stephen, who called upon God and saying "Lord Jesus, receive my spirit." And he kneeled down and cried with a loud voice "Lord lay not this sin to their charge. And when he had said this, he fell asleep."

Acts 7:54-60

Saul The Serial Killer

"And Saul was consenting to his death. And at that time there was a great persecution against the church which was at Jerusalem; and they were all scattered abroad throughout the regions of Judea and Samaria, except the apostles.

I'm Just A Man

And devout men carried Stephen to his burial, and made great lamentation over him. As for Saul, he made havoc of the church, entering into every house, and dragging off men and women (of the faith) and committed them to prison."

Acts 8:1-4

Paul, The Convict

"And it came to pass, as we went to prayer, a certain woman possessed with a spirit of divination met us, which brought her masters much gain by fortune telling. The same followed Paul (formerly known as Saul) and us, and cried saying, "These men are the servants of the most high God, which show unto us the way of salvation." And she did this for many days.

But Paul, being greatly annoyed, turned and said to the spirit, ""I command you in the name of Jesus Christ to come out of her."" And he came out the same hour. And when her masters saw that the hope of their gains was gone, they caught Paul and Silas and dragged them into the market place before the authorities. And brought them to the magistrates, saying "These men, being Jews, do exceedingly trouble our city, and teach customs, which are not lawful for us to receive, neither to observe, being Romans".

And the multitude rose up together against them: and the magistrates tore off their clothes and commanded they be beaten. And when they had laid many stripes on their backs, they threw them into prison, charging the jailer to keep them safely: Who, having received such a charge, threw them into the inner prison and put their feet in stocks."

Acts 16:16-24

REFLECT PROCESS AND JOURNAL

Dr. Casondra R'. Robinson

So……are you a con, ex-con, criminal, unlawful entrepreneur, back room financial advisor, shade tree solicitor or sidewalk business person? Do you suffer from Robin Hood Syndrome, which means stealing from those richer than you for the benefit the poor – namely you, yourself & that person in your bathroom mirror? Well let's meditate on this a moment, shall we?

"If we confess our sins, God is faithful and just to forgive us our sins, and to cleanse us from all unrighteousness."

1 John 1:9

"Temptations that are common to man will come before you: but (remember) God is faithful and will not leave you to forceful temptation beyond your ability, but will always make a way for you to escape and come out on the other side of temptation blameless."

1 Corinthians 10:13

"...hold fast to that which is good. Abstain from all (acts and even the) appearance of evil. And (then) the very God of Peace sanctifies you

completely; and I pray to God your entire spirit and soul and body be preserved blameless in the coming of our Lord Jesus Christ."

1 Thessalonians 5:21-24

"Know therefore that The Lord thy God, He is God, the faithful God which keeps His covenant and mercy with them that love Him and keep His commandments to a thousand generations."

Deuteronomy 7:9

Don't be surprised by what I'm about to tell you: Some of those closest to you will begin to speak bad about you, bringing up your past and how you now think you are better than them; this is called jealousy. Others will recognize that it's not **YOU** who is better, but **YOUR CHARACTER** that has improved for the better (by the grace of God). Those will be the ones who will quietly approach you and ask how to make a change in **Their** life for the better.

Now after reading all of this, you know you ain't got no excuse for not doing right! Begin now to think and speak of your life in a positive light. Don't worry about the people who know the old you;

they had to be in similar lanes to know the route you ran. They may talk about you when they hear you speak differently over your life, but your new behavior will shout them down every time.

I WAS ABUSED AS A CHILD AND CAN'T MOVE PAST IT

Child abuse is never an easy subject. It is, However, a necessary subject, as the world is full of men and women who carry the burden of being abused children.

In the midst of the fear, confusion, a sense of betrayal and pain, things can be turned backwards. One of the most common mistakes we victims of abuse make, is to walk through life carrying a burden that doesn't belong to us.

Your abuse is not a sin that you have to answer to the Lord for. It is the abuser who carries the sin burden which must be answered for. They've put you through enough, don't let them continue to use you, to carry their millstones. Here therefore, is your goal:

BE FREE BELOVED...
...BELOVED BE FREE

Look to God to find your true purpose. It's not about what the world says you'll never be nor accomplish. It's about the ***DESTINY*** God appointed and anointed to you, before you were even in your mother's womb.

I'm Just A Man

Because God is great, His plans for you are also great. Step out of those dark places that you've allowed to fence you in. Stand in the light of the sun and retrain yourself to walk in the light of the holy Son Of God.

God will meet you in the darkest pits and position you over your abusers, misusers, violators, desecrators, every storm that struck you down and every mountain that stood in your way. Want proof? Let me share with you the true story of a boy named Joe.

Joe was the next to the last of a dozen sons. He was the son who brought his daddy the greatest joy. Unlike his older brothers, Joe did whatever his dad asked with great care; obediently and without complaint. Rather than correcting their ways and honoring their daddy, his older brothers simply chose to hate Joe. They taunted, picked at and bullied him every chance they got, especially after he had a dream and dared to share it. But this dream would not be denied, because it foretold of his coming greatness.

Joe's family raised livestock. He was often sent by his daddy to check on his older brothers, who were known to goof off, or laze around when they should have been tending to the animals. Rather than search themselves, they just hated Joe more, calling him their father's spy.

I have children who bring me joy beyond joy. On occasion I like to bless them with things simply because it blesses me to see them enjoy the blessing. I named those days "Just Because Day", because I filled them with wonderful gifts and surprises just because I loved them. How much greater must it bless God to see us enjoy His blessings, which are beyond measure? How much greater the gifts He gives, just because He loves you.

Joe's father, Israel, decided to bless him one day with a beautiful colored coat. Jealousy overtook his brothers and their hatred for him grew beyond the point of reason. What happened next is enough to break anyone's spirit if they don't have faith in God to rely on for their strength.

"And Israel said to Joe, "Aren't your brothers feeding the flock in Shechem? Come and I will send you to them" and he said to him "Here am I." And Israel said "Go, see whether it is well with your brothers and with the flocks: and bring me word again." So he sent him out of the safety of Hebron and he came to Shechem.

And a certain man found him wandering in the field: and asked him

I'm Just A Man

tell me please where they feed their flocks." And the man said, "They are departed hence; for I heard them say they were going to Dothan". "What are you looking for?" And he said, "I'm looking for my brothers, And Joe went after his brothers and found them in Dothan.

And when they saw him coming in the distance they plotted to kill him. And they said one to another, "Behold, this dreamer is coming, come and let's kill him and throw him into some pit, and we will say some ferocious beast has eaten him: and we shall see what becomes of his dreams."

Ruben heard it and tried to save Joe by saying "Let's not kill him. Don't shed his blood, just throw him into this pit that is in the wilderness and don't touch him", that he might deliver him out of their hands and safely back to his father. And it came to pass, when Joe came to his brothers, they stripped him of the coat their father had given him. They threw him into a dry well and sat down to eat bread.

They looked up and saw a company of Ishmaelites from Gilead with their camels bearing spices and balm and myrrh, taking it to Egypt. Judah said to his brothers " do we gain if we kill our brother and hide his blood? Let's sell him to the Ishmaelites and not kill him by our own hand because he is our brother." Then Midianite merchantmen passed by and they lifted Joe out the well and sold him for twenty pieces of silver, and Joe was taken to Egypt as a slave for sale.

Genesis 37:13-28

The brothers took Joe's coat and killed a kid of their goats and dipped the coat in the blood: and they took Joe's coat and brought it to their father and said "We found this, do you recognize this to be Joe's coat?".

Israel, knowing it to be Joe's coat believed that Joe had been devoured by a wild beast, tore his own clothes and could not be consoled. His sons and daughters tried to console him, but he said ""I will go to my grave in mourning for Joe"", and he continued to weep.

Genesis 37:31-35

Joe was not dead but lost to his father, who loved him so very dearly. Many of us are like Joe; lost to our Heavenly Father who then mourns for us, because He loves us beyond measure.

We do have one major advantage over Joe, we can return to the love and protection of God anytime we chose. Even if we have become enslaved to negative thoughts, illicit behaviors or worldly

I'm Just A Man

lifestyles, we can return to Him. It so easy to do, just call Him.

Joe didn't have it that easy. He spent time in Egypt as a slave and was even falsely imprisoned before he stepped into his Destiny. He could have been angry with God and the world, but he wasn't. You see, even though his situation changed, his faith, heart and mindset remained steadfast, unmovable & unshakable.

It is when we remain steadfast in our devotion to and belief in God's word, that we can weather life's storms, earthquakes, tornados and hurricanes. It was his steadfastness that allowed The Lord to in one day, to take Joe from being an abused child, slave and convict, to the second most powerful man in the world.

"And it came to pass in the morning that Pharaoh's spirit was troubled; and he sent and called for all Egypt's magicians and wise men. Pharaoh told them his dream: but none of them could interpret them for him:

Then the chief butler spoke to Pharaoh, saying, "I do remember my faults this day: Pharaoh was angry with his servants and put me in prison along with the chief baker; and we each dreamed a dream one night, each man dream according to his position within Pharaoh's house.

There was there with us a young man, a Hebrew, servant to the jailer. We told him our dreams and he interpreted them to us, each man according to his dream. And it came to pass, as he interpreted to us, so it was; I was restored to my position, and the baker was hanged."

Pharaoh sent for Joe, and they brought him quickly from the dungeon. He was shaved, bathed, dressed in fresh clothes and brought before Pharaoh. Pharaoh said to Joe, "I have dreamed a dream and there is non that can interpret it; and I have heard that you can understand the meaning of dreams."

Joe answered Pharaoh, saying "It is not in me; God shall give Pharaoh an answer of peace." And Pharaoh said to Joe, "In my dream..."

Genesis 41:8-17

Joe interprets that the Pharaoh's dreams are warnings from God of an upcoming natural disaster. Joe not only interpreted the dreams but gave Pharaoh a solution to how they could avoid the disaster, save the kingdom, enrich his coffers and put all other kingdoms at his mercy.

I'm Just A Man

The lesson here to the steadfast is that God's set ups are never small. Don't believe me? Check out what happens next...

"And Pharaoh said to Joe, forasmuch as God has showed you all this, there is none so discerning and wise as you. You shall be over my house, and according to your word shall all my people be ruled; Only in the throne will I be greater than you.

And then Pharaoh said to Joe, See, I have set you over all the land of Egypt. Then Pharaoh took off his ring and put it on Joe's hand, and he dressed him in royal robes of fine linen and put a gold chain around his neck; he made him ride in the second chariot which he had and they cried before him, "Bow the knee;"

Pharaoh made him ruler over all the land of Egypt. Pharaoh said to Joe, I am Pharaoh and without your permission no man shall lift up his hand or foot in all the land of Egypt. Pharaoh changed Joe's name to Zaphnath-paaneah (meaning – God speaks and He lives) and gave him Asenath, the daughter of Potipherah, priest of On as his wife.

So Joe went out over all the land of Egypt and he was only thirty years old when he stood before Pharaoh King of Egypt..."

Genesis 41:39-46

Dr. Casondra R'. Robinson

Can I get a witness that you don't have to be ancient, to be anointed? God does not measure us by the length of our years, but by the measure of our faith. There are a lot of folks older than prehistoric dirt who swear God doesn't make a move without checking their schedule first. Here's a new phrase boys and girls: can you say "dusty ol' hell bound heathen"? Very good! They're usually easy to spot because:

They're under the impression that church can't start without them
…sitting on their self-appointed pew
…trying to lead the church in singing a song
…that they made up on the way there
…wearing a battery operated flashing "Jesus" necktie
…or hat so big it causes a solar eclipse
…neck weighed down with big ol' wall hanging crosses
…wallet full of matches from the "Crystal Pistol Motel"
…right next to the casino "Platinum Member" card
…doing a made up dance they had their cousin Poo choreograph
(that boy got sugar in his veins but he sho' can dance)
…so they could put Sister Essie in her place

I'm Just A Man

Am I rambling a tirade? Well, some of you get the picture, and those who don't, you know there is no way I could be talking about YOU.... anyway.... moving right along...

"And the seven years of famine began to come, according as Joe had said; and the famine was in all lands, but in all the land of Egypt there was bread."

Genesis 41:54

"And Joe was the governor over the land, and it was he that sold to all the people of all the lands; and Joe's older brothers came and bowed down before him with their faces in the dirt."

Genesis 42:6

"And Joe knew his brothers, but they knew him not."

Genesis 42:8

Don't tell me Jehovah is not a mighty God! It is He who will put you in the position where your enemies and tormentors shall willingly, with fear, need and great trembling bow down before you with their faces in the dirt. It is Jehovah God who can change you and your circumstances so much that your enemies won't even recognize who you are!

Joe said "I know who you are, you're spies!" His brothers addressed him as "My Lord" and swore they were the twelve son's of one man. Joe replied "I think you need a few days in the pokey, there are not twelve of you, only ten". Joe left them in the pit of the pokey for three days and brought them back before them to see what kind of tune they would sing this time.

"On the third day Joe told them "Do this and live; for I fear God. If you are men of truth, leave one of your brothers imprisoned here and take corn back to your family. But, when you return, bring your youngest brother back with you so I can verify what you have told me and your lives will be spared."

The brothers begin to talk amongst themselves saying, "We are very guilty concerning our brother, in that we saw the anguish of his soul, when he pleaded with us and we wouldn't listen, that's why this trouble has come upon us".

And Ruben spoke to them saying, "Did I not tell you not to sin against the child and you refused to listen to me? Therefore, see now that his blood must be paid for." Joe understood every word they said, but they didn't know because he spoke to them through an interpreter. *(Genesis 42:18-23)*

    Joe kept Simeon with him to ensure that when they returned they would bring his mother's second son, Ben back with them. You can understand that he wondered if Ben had suffered at his half-brothers hands the way he had.

  He had their asses loaded with corn and the money they'd paid for the food put back. On the way home they discovered the money and cried the Lord had cursed them for their sin against their brother.

    When they returned home with the money and without Simeon, their father was distraught. When they told him the only way they could buy more food and return with Simeon was if Ben went with them to redeem him, Israel grieved and refused.

    He cried out to them that Ben was all he had left of his beloved Rachel. Her only other child Joe, for whom he still mourned, had been eaten by wild beast. If he were to also lose Ben, he was sure it would be enough to send him to his grave.

    Notice that ain't nobody raised their hand and confessed the truth about what really happened to Joe? Didn't nobody write an anonymous note and slide it under they Daddy's pillow when no one was looking?

Know this about people who like to whip out lies: Those whips have a backlash that will return and beat them mercilessly until they confess the truth. And the longer they hold on to their lies, the greater their reputation as a liar will be once the truth is exposed.

My Great-Grandmother, Mama Lula, was a very wise woman. When she spoke, if you were wise, you would shut your mouth, open your ears, grab a pencil and paper, write it down, take it some place quiet and memorize that thing.

Even her brief saying spoke volumes, which is why I am giving one of her greatest lessons a whole page to itself. On more than one occasion when satan would command his minions (including those with church memberships) to begin spreading lies, I saw Mama simply laugh while sitting and sipping a cup of hot, black coffee and say this:

I'm Just A Man

"Baby, what don't come out in the wash
Will come out in the rinse
Lies spread like wild fire
Before the truth can even get it's pants on
But you better believe and know
That the truth will slow-walk a lie to death every time
Anything that ain't of my God
Can't live in the presence of anything that is."
　　　　　　　　Mrs. Lula James McKeever

I learned a lot from listening to her. You can imagine the thoughts, guilt and regrets they carried in their hearts and minds while stretching their corn as long as they could.

Finally, they could stretch the corn no longer and knew it was time to return to Egypt and its governor.

"And their father, Israel said this, "If it must be so, then do this: take the best fruits of the land with you, and take the man a present, a little honey, spices and myrrh, nuts and almonds.

Give him double the money to replace that which was brought back and carry it in your own hands, in case it was an oversight. Take your brother, arise, go again to the man: And God Almighty give you mercy before him that he may send away your brother, and Ben. If I be bereaved of my children, I am bereaved."

Genesis 43:11-14

Dang! You can imagine how low they felt. And they were still holding on to that lie; and you'd better believe that it was whipping the heck out of them. They followed their father's instructions, saddled up and left for Egypt, each stewing in his own thoughts of

I'm Just A Man

his actions of the past and their present circumstances.

They went again and stood in the dirt before their brother. When Joe saw his brother Ben, he told his chief steward to bring the men to his home and prepare a meal; he would dine with them. The brothers were very afraid because Egyptians thought it was unclean to dine with Hebrews.

They feared it was a trap, that all their possession would be taken and they would be kept as slaves. It was then that jaws got loose and gums got to bumping, trying to save themselves from what would surely be the end of them. They spoke to Joe's steward, trying to get things straight before he got there.

"O sir, we came indeed down the first time to buy food: and when we stopped to camp for the night, somehow every man's money was in his sack to the very penny. We brought it back, plus the money to pay for another load of corn."

The Steward said "Peace be unto you, fear not: your God and the God of your father, has given you treasure in your sacks. I had your money". He then brought Simeon out to them.

The steward took them to Joe's apartments in the Pharaoh's palace, gave them water to wash their feet and feed their animals.

They made ready their gifts in preparation for Joe's coming at noon, because they had been told that he would break bread with them.

When Joe came home, they brought forth his presents and yet again unknowingly fulfilled Joe's long ago prophetic dream by bowing down before the brother they had tormented, abused, mistreated and sold into slavery. He asked them of their welfare and said, "Is your father well, the old man that you spoke of, is he yet alive?" "Thy servant, our father is yet alive" they answered and they bowed their heads and laid out prostrate before him." *(Genesis 43:20-28)*

I have to stop here for a minute just to testify that God will lay your enemies prostrate at your feet! Hallelujah! Glory to Jehovah God who is fair and just and avenges His faithful servants!!

Remember how we talked about God not being a respecter of person? That means that what He did for Joe, He will surely do for you. So go shine every pair of shoes you own; that way when your enemies and tormentors; misusers and abusers bow down & lay prostrate before you, they can see their own miserable faces right before their foreheads hit that dirt.

Excuse me for a moment, but as an abused child I have to stop for a minute and get my praise on…………Whew! It's a shame you missed my dance, it was very cute, but perhaps you did hear my shout. Okay…moving right along…

"Joe looked up and saw his brother Ben, his mother's son and said "Is this your younger brother that you spoke of?"" Then he said "God be gracious unto you my son". And Joe quickly left the room, for his heart yearned for his brother.

He looked for a place to hide his tears, so he went into his Bedroom and wept. Then he washed his face, pulled himself together and went back before his brothers and commanded that the meal begin.

Joseph set apart from them because it was an abomination for Egyptians to eat with Hebrews. Yet, he seated his brothers in the order of their birth, from the oldest to the youngest. They noticed this and marveled at how he knew such a thing." *(Genesis 43:29-33)* Won't God give you inside information that will confuse your enemies?

"Joe sent them servings of food, but to Ben he sent five times as much." The brothers ate, drank and became very merry with the brother they knew not." *(Genesis 43:44)*

I'm Just A Man

"Joe played it real cool because he had a final test to see whether or not his brothers had changed. He told his steward to fill their bags with as much food as they could carry, along with a double portion money they brought. He then told him to put his own silver cup into Ben's bag.

The next morning the eleven brothers were on their way back home when Joe's soldiers, lead by his steward overtook them as said as his master told him to: "Why have you rewarded good with evil? Where is the cup you stole; The one from which my lord drank and knows that you have done this evil?"

The brothers protested saying, "Why does my lord say these words? God forbid that we, his servants should do such a thing! (Notice how Joe's abusers are referring to themselves as his servants? My, My, My….what a difference a day makes) We brought back the money that was put in our sacks the first time we came, so why should we now steal silver or gold from thy lord's house?"

Then they got cocky and with their mouths wrote a check their behinds couldn't cash; "Among whichever one of us you find the cup, let him die and the remainder of us will be your lord's slaves!"
(Genesis 44:3-9)

Dr. Casondra R'. Robinson

"Don't you dig a hole for God's child
Unless you dig two
The first hole His child will rise from
The second hole will capture you"

Mrs. Lula James McKeever

Boy, my Great-Grandmother was one wise woman! Any opportunity you have to hear the wisdom of an aged saint, take it. If you do most of the listening, instead of the majority of talking, you'll leave much wiser than you came. Thank God for the wisdom of our elders in His word!

"The steward quickly said, "Let it be as you say, but like this; the one found with my master's cup shall be my slave and the remainder of you shall return home blameless." Each man quickly unloaded his sack, put it on the ground and opened it. The steward searched each man's bag, starting with the oldest and ending with the youngest. The cup was found in Ben's bag.

The brothers tore their clothes in mourning, loaded their bags back on their donkeys and returned to the city. When they reached Joe's house, he was there waiting for them and said, "What deed have you done that I would not know about?" (hmmm….I wonder..…..)

Judah said "What can we say to you? What words can we speak to clear our names? God has uncovered our sin and now we are your servants, the ten of us and the one in whose sack the cup was found."

Joe said "God forbid that I should keep any as my slave but the one found guilty. You innocent ones go in peace and return again to your father." Judah came before Joe and said, "Oh my lord, let your servant speak a word into your ear, and do not be angry with me for you are as mighty as Pharaoh.

You asked us if we had a father or a brother. We told you we have a father, an old man and a child of his old age, a little one, and his brother is dead and he alone is left of his mother and our father loves him. And then you told us to bring him down so you could see him and we told you he cannot leave his father, for if he should leave his father, his father will die.

But you said that unless we bring him we would never see your face again. When we reached my father, we told him of your words.

Dr. Casondra R'. Robinson

When our father told us to come again to buy a little food, we reminded him you would not see us unless we brought our little brother.

You servant, my father, said "you know that my wife bore me two sons. One went out from me and I said surely he has been eaten by wild beast and I have not seen him since. If you take this remaining one from me and any harm should befall him, it will bring my gray hairs to my grave with sorrow."

So now, when I return to my father without the boy, seeing that his life is intertwined with the boy's life, he will die and we, your servants, shall be the cause of our father, your servant, going down into his grave with great sorrow.

I stood as a guarantee for the boy to my father, that if I do not return with him, I shall bear the blame forever. Therefore, I beg of you, let me remain with you in the place of my brother as your slave.

Let him leave with my brothers, because how can I return to my father without him, and watch the doom that shall come to my father?"

His brothers ways had changed and Joe could keep himself from them no longer. He ordered all his servants from the room. When there was no one left but Joe and his brothers, Joe wept so loud that the Egyptians and the house of Pharaoh heard him sobbing.

To his brothers he said, "I am Joseph, is my father still alive?" His brothers couldn't answer because they were terrified. He said "come closer" and when they came closer he told them "I am Joseph, your brother whom you sold as a slave into Egypt". *(Genesis 44:10 – 45:4)*

Have you ever seen someone who just **KNEW** they were looking and smelling good? Everywhere they walked people stared and stepped aside; and they (with their *fiiine* self) nodded to them graciously, with eyes that said "I know, I know, but try not to go blind in the radiance of my goodlookedness".

Oh yeah Beloved...they had it going on!!! That is until they passed a store window... looked in the glass and saw a tore up hot mess.

Now at their very first glance, they thought to themselves "tsk, tsk, tsk that poor creature… bless 'em Lord to at least *do* better, if not look better." Then they noticed the creature looking at them the same way.

Their indignation, suddenly changed to mortification, when they realized that tore up hot mess in the window was them! The humidity had humiliated their hair, dressing in the dark had their clothes on inside out and wait a minute…the wind just changed… that bird bath they took… well, it didn't take (now you know they knew they were bigger than a bird when they first got to splashing).

Tsk, tsk, tsk that poor creature…may The Lord bless them to at least *do* better, if not look better. You see, thinking their cover up was complete, they left home acting all vain, now they're running around looking all insane. Why? I'll tell you why: Because...

"You can't play in the devil's dirt
without walking away covered in what you thought was dirt
but was really a lot of dirt-colored stuff
with a strong stank that you didn't smell
until you started moving it around!"

Me

Can you imagine the thoughts that ran through his older brother's minds? He was no longer a boy over which they had the brute strength and number to abuse. God had taken that abused little boy and placed him in such a position of power, that with a word he could destroy them and their families in a million different ways.

They remembered every foul deed they committed against him, every lie they ever told to cover their actions. They realized that every moment they had stood before their brother, the second most powerful man in the entire world, they stood stank with their clothes on inside out. They stood before him with the tables now turned. It was now they who were helpless, exposed and at their brother's absolute mercy.

We, who have been abused, have often dreamed of the things we would do, if we had absolute power over our abusers. Perhaps I should speak only for myself and say that since I was four years old, I've had such dreams.

Over the years, as I grew; not only did my appearance change, but my dreams changed also. You see, I know now that it was God, who not only gave me the strength to survive, but a life worth living. Every time the Lord in His mercy lifted my broken heart and battered body, He healed, strengthened, nurtured and matured my character.

Dr. Casondra R' Robinson

He did it through the words and songs of my maternal Grandparents and Great-Grandmother, two of my paternal Aunts who loved me like mothers and their husbands, the Uncles who didn't love me like a niece, but as if I were their daughter.

I can't forget my childhood Pastors, a Sunday School teacher, a Red Circle leader, a Pastor's Choir director who would not allow me to sing a hymn unless I truly understood the meaning of the song, and many other saints of God that the Lord directed in my path.

Never underestimate the tenacity, the life span of the seeds you sow into children. It took all of these people being obedient to God, to help me to become the person I am today.

Decades ago I asked forgiveness from those I offended by acting out as angry children do; and forgave all of my abusers in my heart. I sincerely forgave them, which allowed me to finally walk away from the pain. If any of my abusers are reading this, I need you to know that God loves you. If you have not repented of your past sins, it's not too late. If you have not changed your ways and are still breathing, IT'S NOT TOO LATE.

God will forgive you, but only if you sincerely ask it; the hard part will be seeking the forgiveness of those you've harmed, and last but not least, you must forgive yourself. We can all be like Joseph; allowing God to change our position in life for the better and refusing to let satan to keep our emotions tied up in dark places.

Joe spoke to them again, "'Do not be afraid or angry with yourselves for selling me here. God has used your deed for the benefit of preserving our lives. The famine has lasted two years and there are still five to follow. The God of Abraham positioned me here in order to preserve a remnant of Isaac and to save your lives by a deliverance that only He can get the glory for.

Although you in your sin, sold me here – it was God who made me a father to Pharaoh, and lord of all of his house and a ruler throughout all the land of Egypt." *(Genesis 45:5-8)*

"Lord, you prepare a table for me in the presence of my enemies…"

Psalms 23:5

"And Israel took his journey with all that he had, and came to Beer-Sheba and offered sacrifices unto the God of his father, Isaac. And God spoke to Israel in visions of the night and said "Jacob, Jacob" and he said "Here am I."

Dr. Casondra R'. Robinson

And he said "I am God, the God of your father: do not be afraid to go down into Egypt for it is there that I will make you a great nation. I will go down with you into Egypt and I will also surely bring you up again: and Joseph shall put his hand upon your eyes."

And Jacob rose up from Beer-Sheba and the sons of Israel carried Jacob, their father, and their little ones, and their wives, in the wagons which Pharaoh had sent to carry him.

And they took their cattle, and their goods, which they had gotten in the land of Canaan, and came into Egypt, Jacob and all his seed with him: His sons, and his son's sons with him, his daughters, and his son's daughters, and all his seed brought he with him to Egypt."

Genesis 46:1-7

"And Joseph made ready his chariot, and went up to meet Israel, his father, to Goshen, and presented himself to him; and he fell on his neck, and wept on his neck a good while."

Genesis 46:29

I'm Just A Man

Praise Break!! Hallelujah to God Almighty, who is the God of restoration! Hosanna to Jehovah who brings restoration to us even now, when we can imagine it not! Glory! Worthy is He who not only restores but redeems………..Whew!…I had to do my dance, wait a minute……….I thought I was finished, but I still had a few cute steps left in me that I just had to get out! Moving right along…

"And Pharaoh said to Joseph: ""Your father and your brothers have come to you. The land of Egypt is before you, make your father and brothers to live in the best of Egypt's land, in Goshen.

If you know of any among them who are competent, make them rulers over my cattle."" Then Joseph brought in Jacob, his father, before Pharaoh and Jacob blessed Pharaoh.

And Pharaoh said to Jacob, "How old are you?" And Jacob answered the days of the years of my pilgrimage are a hundred and thirty years: few and evil have the days of the years of my life been, and have not attained unto the days of the years of the life of my fathers in the days of their pilgrimage. And Jacob blessed Pharaoh and went out from before him."

Genesis 47:5-10

Dr. Casondra R'. Robinson

Israel lived another seventeen years in the care of his beloved son Joseph, who loved him dearly.

REFLECT PROCESS AND JOURNAL

Dr. Casondra R' Robinson

Whew! That was some chapter huh? Well abuse is some subject. Let me begin by saying to those of you who were ever abused in any way…

"I AM SO VERY SORROWFUL THAT YOU SUFFERED SUCH EGREGIOUSNESS. ABUSE IN ANY FORM IS WRONG AND MY HEART GRIEVES FOR THE CHILD IN YOU."

As a child of abuse, I am beyond sympathy, I empathize with you. But this one thing I do know; that if I can move past it...so can you. The same God that enabled me to do so, also moves in your life.

> "Then Peter opened his mouth, and said, Of a truth I perceive that God is no respecter of persons: But in every nation he that feareth him, and worketh righteousness, is accepted with Him.
>
> *Acts 10:34-35*

So is there an experience from your past that still leaves you with a sour taste? Remember; what the enemy means for your downfall, our God will use for your uplifting.

You might not want to hear this, but you have to forgive everyone who ever hurt you. Forgiveness is not for them, forgiveness is for **YOU**. As long as you have a wall of unforgiveness between you and God, all interaction between you is blocked by the wall.

Your forgiveness for your sins is blocked by that wall. Your prayers are blocked by that wall. Your blessings, favor, mercy, grace, increase, harvest, promotion, etc., are blocked by that wall.

Once you forgive, you are able to release the anger, horror, pain, betrayal, fear, anxiety, sorrow, etc. The goal is to release every offense of man, keeping only God's gift of the lesson that He sent to make you wiser.

God always puts a lesson in the midst of the pain caused by man, to imprint into your mind the familiarity of that type of demon spirit. God knows that until you defeat it, it will keep returning to you, just wearing different skins.

The lesson leads you to study scripture on abolishing that spirit, teaches you to recognize it and gives you the tools to banish it, thus no longer be trapped by within it's cycle of pain.

Dr. Casondra R'. Robinson

Here's a 5 step plan that may work for you:

1) Draw a picture of a lemon

2) Write on it every experience that left that sour taste in your mouth Draw more lemons if needed

3) Find a safe place to build a contained fire

4) Put the lemon(s) in the fire

5) As you watch the paper begin to burn, tell those thoughts and feelings about the negative emotions, thoughts and relationships you gained by keeping them

6) Tell them the positive emotions, thoughts and relationships you lost or were denied by keeping them

7) Tell them you are revoking their right to reside within you ever again

8) As the smoke rises, release everything you wrote to God with the following prayer:

I'm Just A Man

A Prayer Of Forgiveness And Release

Father God, in the name of Jesus, I need You
I need You to help me start anew
I forgive any and all who have sinned against me
Please forgive me for any and all sins I have committed against You
Forgive me Lord, for any and all sins I have committed against others
Be forgiving Father, for any and all sins I have committed against myself
I forgive myself, for any and all sins I have committed against myself
Release me from the shackles that bind me
Free me from the burdens put upon my body, mind and spirit
Free me from the burdens I have put upon myself
My soul is cold
Cover me with the warm blanket of Your righteousness
Take me as I am
Let me be one of those whom You love, provide for and protect
I am Yours, Lord Jesus, to command
Amen – Amen – Amen

Don't take it back! Trust and know in accordance with His word, God will work with it in your favor. Watch your Daddy as He adds Living Water, sugar and ice. He'll stir it up real good, and even add an umbrella and curly straw. Then He'll give it back to you to drink in the presence of your tormentors, in the middle of their heat wave!

Continue to say this prayer however long it takes to overcome the issues of your past. And always remember that God is faithful, and He has a heart for those who have become His children in the faith.

I KNOW

I'M CALLED

I JUST AIN'T

ANSWERING

THE PHONE

Dr. Casondra R'. Robinson

How many times have you heard the words "God's got a calling on your life."? How many times has God showed you your purpose, and you ran in the other direction? How many times has He spared your life, while you were busy running in that other direction? When do you plan on "answering the phone"?

A FEW REASONS PEOPLE USE TO RUN FROM GOD
(Not you of course)

I'M TOO YOUNG...

When Samuel was a mere child, God sent him the first vision that began his journey to becoming high priest.

> *"Now the boy Samuel ministered to the LORD before Eli. And the word of the LORD was rare in those days; there was no widespread revelation. And it came to pass at that time, while Eli was lying down in his place, and when his eyes had begun to grow so dim that he could not see, and before the lamp of God went out in the tabernacle[a] of the LORD where the ark of God was, and while Samuel was lying down, that the LORD called Samuel..."*
>
> 1 Samuel 3:1-4

I'm Just A Man

I'M TOO OLD...

Abraham was one hundred years old and Sarah was 90 when Isaac was conceived and born.

"And the LORD visited Sarah as He had said, and the LORD did for Sarah as He had spoken. For Sarah conceived and bore Abraham a son in his old age, at the set time of which God had spoken to him."

Genesis 21:1-2

I'M NOT ACADEMICALLY/SEMINARY EDUCATED...

I am a witness that God does not always call the educated, but He always educates those whom He calls.

Me

PEOPLE KNOW MY PAST, WHO WOULD LISTEN?...

Those who seek or have a curiosity concerning Christ will listen to you.

"The Samaritan woman ran through the city telling the men "Come see a man who told me everything I've ever done. Is this not the Christ?"

Dr. Casondra R'. Robinson

Then they went out of the city and came to Him"

John 4:29-30

I DON'T WANT PEOPLE TO THINK I'M A JESUS NUT...
"Tis better to be a nut
That's fastened on to the right bolt
Than to be found by The Carpenter
Screwed up, over and around"

Me

MY FAMILY/FRIENDS WON'T SUPPORT ME
God will send your supporters

"...Jesus said to Simon, ""Fear not; from this day forward you shall catch men." And when then brought their ships to land, they gave up all they had and followed him."

Luke 5:11

Do we have to be thrown overboard in a hurricane, swallowed by a whale and wallow in the acid of its belly for three days before God gets our undivided attention?

I'm Just A Man

Will we only find solid ground, when we're a particle of fish vomit? Sounds nasty, don't it? That's cause it is...now wash that up-chuck off, fry you a king sized fish plate and go in the direction God commands you. Don't walk Beloved...drop that excuse and run!

REFLECT PROCESS AND JOURNAL

I'm Just A Man

So, Dear Heart...how much longer will you wrongly invest in pretending to be what you were not created to be? How much longer will you run away from your Creator? Write below what it is about the road to your Destiny that seems so intimidating/frightening.

1. _____
2. _____
3. _____
4. _____
5. _____
6. _____
7. _____
8. _____
9. _____
10. _____.

Now, let's get to rebuking with the following prayer, shall we?

Dr. Casondra R'. Robinson

Father God, I come before you today in prayer
Although there is joy in your presence, there is sorrow in my heart
I feel discouraged, incapable, unable, not enough
That I have no right to be who You created me to be
Take the voices of self-doubt from me
Void my every excuse to not serve you
I give them to you right now
I rebuke them from re-entering my heart & mind
I will daily work to fulfill the DESTINY You gave me
I will daily meditate on the purposeful plan I received from You
When the enemy tries to retell those lies concerning who I am
Embolden & aide me to remember the might of my two-edged sword
that you sharpened with the word and placed behind my lips
Train me, make me strong to resist;
That I may one day stand in the position to help others
To likewise resist he who defiles
I put my faith in You, ready to do the work that will enact it
Thank you Lord, for this and all things of and from You
In Jesus' name – Amen – Amen – Amen

AND FINALLY…

Dr. Casondra R'. Robinson

What To Do When The Lord Speaks

Go where God tells you to go
Move like He tells you to move
Be still when He says "Hold and see my salvation"
Do what He tells you to do
Say what He tells you to say
Only to whom He tells you to say it to
But close your mouth if He tells you to be quiet
Don't get mad if things don't have the effect you want
And don't take the credit if water springs from a dry rock
It's not about you
It's not about your plan
It's about GOD
It's about HIS PLAN
And HIS PURPOSE
And trust…He has a DESTINY, a purposeful plan for us all.
Now go and live in complete obedience to God.
And as you begin your journey
Allow me to pray a Prophet's Blessing over you:

I'm Just A Man

A Prophet's Blessing

May the Lord God bless and sustain you
May He keep His healing hand of grace and mercy over your life
May every morning you bear witness to new miracles
May you daily seek His face, hear and obey His voice
May everything taken from you be restored
May everything added to you be in abundance
May you slumber and arise each day resting on pillows of His assurance
May your journey and labor end at the feet of The Master
May you hear Him call you "Servant" and say "Well done"
I bless you in the name of the One who took off His crown of Majesty
I bless you in the name of the One who put on man's crown of thorns
I bless you in the name of the One who died taking to Himself our agony
I bless you in the name of the One who arose in victory
Ascending to our Father and now advocating on our behalf
I bless you in the name of Jesus Christ, Amen – Amen – Amen

Just A Man In Jesus Christ,
Prophet Casondra R'. Robinson, Th.D., Ph.D.

RESOURCES FOR INNER FREEDOM

I'm Just A Man

My first recommendation is to get the ultimate source of answers, encouragement and comfort; a bible whose language you can understand.

Find a solid faith based church that teaches the word, not personal opinions. Settle in and study so that you can grow in knowledge, understanding and wisdom.

"This also comes from The Lord of Host which is wonderful in counsel and excellent in working (towards your purpose)."

Isaiah 28:29

If you are a victim of abuse, no matter how long ago, no matter the form it took i.e. physical, verbal, mental, emotional, sexual or other – get licensed Christian Counseling, which is immensely different from having a licensed counselor who is also a Christian.

"Where no counsel is, the people fall; but in the multitude of counselors there is safety."

Proverbs 11:14

Dr. Casondra R'. Robinson

Even if you think you've buried it so deep that it doesn't affect you and those around you, do it. It's a secretive poison that can slowly cripple and kill the best of YOU from the inside out. This is why I recommend faith based counseling that is founded and centered on the word of God. After all, who knows you better than the One who created you?

"Without counsel (your) purposes (plans) are uncompleted but in the multitude of counselors plans are established."

Proverbs 15:22

If you can not find a licensed Christian Counselor, call or contact NAMI, the National Alliance on Mental Illness for help. Don't be thrown off by the words mental illness. You don't have to be a professional underwater basket weaver to call and they can assist you in your search.

"...but he that heeds counsel is wise"

Proverbs 12:15

I'm Just A Man

NAMI not only directs you to licensed Christian Counselors who specialize in your situation, they also offer state and local resources for additional help. Don't worry, their files are kept confidential.

"Hear counsel and receive knowledge that you will be wise in you later plans."

Proverbs 19:20

God created you with a DIVINE DESTINY, a purposeful plan for your life that's worth fighting for.

"Every purpose is established with counsel, and with good advice make war."

Proverbs 20:18

National Alliance on Mental Illness (NAMI)
3803 N. Fairfax Drive, Suite 100
Arlington, VA 22203
Information Helpline – 1-800-950-NAMI (6424)
www.nami.org

ABOUT THE AUTHOR

Dr. Casondra Robinson is a multi-talented Pastor, Theologian, CEO, Christian Counselor, Life Coach, Author, Speaker and Radio Personality. She is called "The Destiny Road Warrior" for her intrinsic ability to help others discover and reach their DESTINY, God's perfect and purposeful plan for their lives.

Her communication methodology is imaginative and humorous, but thought provoking. Using a mixture of true life experiences, parables and outrageously funny antidotes, Dr. Robinson connects with crowds on an individual, intimately personal level.

Holding a Doctorate Degrees in Family Ministry, Ph.D., Theology, Th.D., Christian Counseling, Ph.D., along with her Doctorate of Letters, Litt.D., she is CEO of Sacred Gethsemane Chapel Ministries, Inc., Sacred Trust Christian Counseling, Inc., and Destiny Road Warrior, Inc., among other ventures.

Her favorite scripture is an amalgamation of the first four words of Genesis 1:1 and the last word of Revelation 22:21; "In the beginning God" and that FINAL "Amen".

When asked why, she replied "Because at the beginning of every event of my life, good and bad, God was with me. So at the end of each event, good and bad, I must always remember to glorify Him, praising His plan for my life, which will end – and begin anew – with that final "Amen".

www.ingramcontent.com/pod-product-compliance
Lightning Source LLC
LaVergne TN
LVHW051558070426
835507LV00021B/2645